INTRODUCTION
TO
THE FUTURE

by
Randall L. Scheel

An ETC Publication

Library of Congress Cataloging in Publication Date

Scheel, Randall L., 1952 -
Introduction to the Future

1. Forecasting. I. Title.
CB158.S285   1987   303.4'9   86-16632
ISBN 0-88280-101-5

Published by ETC Publications
Palm Springs
California 92263-1608

CONTENTS

CHAPTER 1

THE NATURE OF CHANGE AND ALTERNATIVE FUTURES

A Time of Change

Under the impact of forces that have generated tremendous change in recent decades, we now seem closer to the future than to the past. We seem torn between our heritage, which is so closely recorded and often cherished, and the future, which lies ahead promising greater and more decisive changes. Some foresee a future of promise and others see peril, but nearly all of us anticipate uncertainty and change as the dominant features of the future.

In 1965 Alvin Toffler coined the term "future shock" to describe what occurs to the individual when he or she is subjected to rapid change in too short a time. Disorientation sets in when our culture undergoes rapid change. Contemporary times, with all its shocks and surprises, can induce a feeling of apprehensiveness. This can culminate in alienation from the entire society to a point where we become apathetic, which is nurtured by a sense of powerlessness or insignificance in the face of accelerated change.

Recent psychological studies have indicated that not only a high rate of change can generate stress but a low rate may also contribute to the problem. It seems that both too much change and not enough change can cause a greater impact than change that we perceive as desirable.

What are some significant changes and when have they occurred? It may help in answering if you imagine yourself going back in time one hundred years. Imagine that you get arrested and after emptying your pockets you realize what a commotion you have caused. They want to know why you carry so many keys and you have to explain the automobile. They want to know what the plastic card is and you attempt to explain credit and the consumer society. They want to know what the pills are and you try to explain aspirin and all the "wonder drugs" of your era. Before long you find yourself engaged in a lengthy discussion of the energy crisis, the workings of modern economics, the moral issues of biomedicine and all to the total amazement and disbelief of your listeners.

Within just one generation, since World War II, we have witnessed more technological change than all of recorded history. The acceleration of this change becomes evident when we compare the time lag between invention and application. It took 112 years for photography to go from discovery to the widely accepted camera, 56 years for the telephone, 35 years for radio, 15 years for radar, 12 years for television, six years for the atomic bomb, and five years for the transister to go from the laboratory to the radio.

Change is not limited to technology; change influences many aspects of social life as well. In the period since 1945, we have seen 85 new nations appear, and the world population has doubled from approximately two billion to four billion. The gross world product (GWP), accounting for all the goods and services produced, has increased even more rapidly. These dynamic forces have acted upon each other to mold a world that will be radically different from anything we have known in the past. The momentum allows us to be consciously aware of what is occurring in the home, the workplace, the freeway, the school, the military, the government, and the entire global structure as never before. Each new machine, concept, and idea interacts with all the others to compel even more change in a system that feeds upon itself. They, in turn, alter the global structure. Each new invention creates new ideas, new ways of looking at our global village. New ideas create new inventions, new inventions create new ideas . . . ad infinitum at an ever accelerating pace. There are now over four billion human beings on our planet, everyone of us unique. Each of us have our own mindscape so there are over four billion visions of reality. Each of these mental perceptions are the sum of the individual's personal life experiences, values, and goals. Your mindscape is of central importance as it has a tremendous influence on how you view human nature and our future. Just as Earth's landscape consists of a multitude of different components, is always being affected by external factors, and constantly evolving, so too is the human mindscape. It influences your action in the present which sets your course into the future. It is the mindscapes of today that will create the realities of tomorrow.

We increasingly feel another aspect of change—obsolescence. It seems that with the development of something new, something old becomes outdated. According to some estimates, half of what an engineer learns in engineering school is out of date seven years after graduation. Computer programmers, much in demand in the sixties and seventies, may find that many of their skills will no longer be needed because many computers may program themselves. Pharmacists find they must go back to school, since seven out of ten prescriptions were unknown thirty years ago. One drug company executive has said, "We used to have one major advance about every twenty-five years. Now we have one every twenty-four hours."

All of these elements comprise a dramatic change in culture, a modification in the way people live. In prehistoric times cultures changed very slowly, and entire generations lived much the same as previous ones. While change intensified over centuries of time, it has been only within the last few decades that there has been a serious need for future studies, for in static societies there is little incentive and need to look ahead. The greater the acceleration of change, the less time there is to anticipate and fully prepare for their implications.

The generation gap, which was never particularly explosive in earlier and more stable times, is now a major source of tension in society. In a rapidly changing society young people grow up in an environment that is dramatically different from their parents. While their behavior, attitudes, and values may be different from that of the older generation, it is more often simply a form of adapting and progressing with the times. The younger generation senses that this lifetime of change is unparalleled in its scale and scope of change. History has recorded other periods of upheaval, but these were usually contained within geographic or societal borders. Today, as Toffler states, ". . . the network of social ties is so tightly woven that the consequences of contemporary events radiate instantaneously around the world."

Future shock is significant in that it forces us to recognize the importance of change and how it is going to shape the future. But are we to be overwhelmed by it, possibly to the point of taking on a reactionary outlook? Should we be afraid of the future and seek to avoid it? No. Instead we must develop a bold new philosophy of the future. A realistic assessment of the new imperative is given by Eric Hoffer: "We can never be really prepared for that which is wholly new. We have to adjust ourselves, and every radical adjustment is a crisis of self-esteem. . . . It needs inordinate self-confidence to face drastic change without inner trembling." This self-confidence can help people to want to face the future. Rapid change in our world is making self-confidence a major prerequisite to a satisfactory personal future.

It is reassuring to consider how adaptable the human being actually is. We are born equipped with a wide range of adaptive potentialities which, combined with long-range plans and guidelines, can help steer us through the future. This is not to say that we should blindly accept or encourage change solely for the sake of change but rather that we should strive to guide our forward thrust. We can find comfort in the realization that many things do not change over time and therefore give us at least a minimum of stability and permanence. These human constants include love, honesty, beauty, truth, and other attributes of the human condition. It can only be hoped that if history must repeat itself, that it does so in a manner which includes these human constants, and not those that bring about war and other human misery.

Future shock does permeate our society and often tends to rudely invade our consciousness, but it must be viewed in a larger scope. We are adaptable, many things do not change, and change may break down undesirable norms and institutions. To quote Raymond Fletcher, a member of the British Parliament: "All these alarming symptoms that so frighten us—they may be birth symptoms instead of death symptoms."

Seven Change Factors

Developed by the Center for Adaptive Learning, the following grouping, while not being the only ones, represent different types of change that operate in all societies.

1. *Demographic.* In any society differences in population growth generate other changes.

2. *Technological innovation.* Changes in technology trigger other changes.

3. *Social innovation.* New arrangements, systems, or styles within the basic social, political, and economic structures will generate change.

4. *Cultural-value shifts.* Changes in culture and values will trigger other changes.

5. *Ecological shifts.* Any major change in the natural environment may cause changes in human society.

6. *Information-idea shifts.* New knowledge will generate societal changes.

7. *Cultural diffusion.* A transfer of ideas, values, or techniques from one culture to another, while taking the form of any of the other change factors, will generate change.

Advance Societal Indicators of Change

Historical analysis has led Willis W. Harman in *An Incomplete Guide to the Future* to conclude that there has usually been certain advance indicators that appear one to three decades before a major change becomes apparent. The fall of the Roman Empire; the Protestant Reformation; the Industrial Revolution; the political revolutions in England, America, and France, and the communist revolution in Russia were all preceded by the following lead indicators:

● Alienation, purposelessness, lowered sense of community.

● Increased rate of mental disorders, violent crime, social disruptions, use of police to control behavior.

● Increased public acceptance of hedonistic behavior (particularly sexual), of symbols of degradation, of lax public morality.

● Heightened interest in noninstitutionalized religious activities (e.g., cults, revivals, secret practices).

● Signs of anxiety about the future, economic inflation (in some cases).

As we approach the next century and apply these indicators to the present, can you help but wonder what major changes the future holds? Will these indicators perpetuate themselves until we reach a stage of societal breakdown or will they prove to be blessings in disguise? If they are ever to be seen as blessings, it will be because we did not ignore them, but instead addressed ourselves to them with the full attention and intelligence they deserve.

The Legitimacy Challenge

Again, drawing from Harman's *An Incomplete Guide to the Future,* we are presented with the theory that within the last ten to fifteen years, the industrialized world has experienced a challenge to its legitimacy. History indicates that the most powerful impetus for social change has been societal challenge to the established order by questioning its legitimacy. According to Harman, the following signs indicate a trend toward legitimacy challenge:

● Third World insistence on a new international economic order.

● Environmentalist, consumer, minority rights, women's liberation, and youth protest movements.

● Criticisms of industrial products, business practices, and manipulative advertising.

● Survey data showing values and attitudes that imply need for change in the world order.

● Growing sense that old answers no longer work.

● Indications of disenchantment with the assumption that all scientific and technological advance is unqualifiedly good.

● Decreased trust in institutions of business and government.

● New labor demands for meaningful work and participation in management decisions.

● Increasing signs of alienation from work and from the non-communities called cities and suburbs.

● Evidence of widespread search for transcendental meanings to provide a sense of "what is worth doing."

Science Fiction

We often hear talk about the Good Old Days when life was supposedly simple and predictable. Whether one yearns for those days or finds a sense of relief for not having to live in

11

them, we all must look to the future and contemplate change and how it shapes the world. Due to today's revolutionary speed of change, it has become imperative that we learn how to influence these changes and create an environment in which desirable change can flourish. It is here, at this point, that science fiction finds its role.

H. Bruce Franklin, who teaches science fiction at Rutgers University and is the author of *Future Perfect*, defines science fiction as ". . . the one genre able to relate the developments of science and technology and our senses of the future with our individual lives and our lives as a society."

The Industrial Revolution, which brought industrialization and technology into the forefront of our lives, motivated Jules Verne to speculate on the implications of this new order in life. Verne, a Frenchman, began studying science after working in other fields and eventually wrote a paper on controlling balloon flight. It was suggested that he make an adventure story out of it and *Five Weeks in a Balloon*, written in 1863, sent him on a new career. By the time of his death in 1903, he had written about sixty books.

Verne's books were well researched and based on the latest scientific findings of the time. His work paid off. One of the characters in *From the Earth to the Moon* suggested using aluminum as the main component for the projectile. In Verne's day this was almost unheard of since aluminum was then considered a rare metal and was consequently very expensive. His research had proven to him that it had the necessary qualities for such application and today, due in part of his farsighted research, it is in common use. What is more, Verne's fictitious flight to the Moon ended in a mid-ocean splashdown, just as Apollo 8 did a century later. Frank Borman, the commander of the mission, wrote a letter to Verne's grandson proclaiming the writer as "one of the great pioneers of the space age."

12

The nineteenth century began with the invention of the locomotive and ended with the airplane and automobile. These dramatic strides were reflected in the writings of many American authors of that time who recognized that these changes, rooted in science and technology, were responsible for changing the quality of life in the United States. While not at the time recognized as science fiction, these literary works are now considered the foundation of a separate branch of literature. By dealing with the implications of science and technology, these writers were trying to describe the reality of what surrounded them.

By the 1930's the world had been introduced to the future by many authors, but perhaps the most noted was H.G. Wells. Long recognizing the importance of the future, he noted "It is into the future we go: tomorrow is the eventful thing for us." Perhaps best known for such masterpieces of fiction as *The Time Machine* and *War of the Worlds,* he also wrote about the future in nonfiction terms as in *Anticipations* in 1901. Here he dealt with the changes in transportation, communication, and warfare. Speaking in a more serious line in *The Outline of History,* he wrote "Human history becomes more and more a race between education and catastrophe." During the 1930's, an English group, the Science Fiction Association, began publishing *Tomorrow: The Magazine of the Future,* which Wells helped support. Its life was short though, as World War II arrived and its founders went off to war. It ended with a development that Wells foresaw in a 1913 novel, *The World Set Free.* The development was the atomic bomb.

Fueled by wartime technology, science fiction found itself in the 1950's and 1960's, a period which has been referred to as the golden age of science fiction. Isaac Asimov, author of over two hundred books, both fiction and nonfiction, recalls, "After the dropping of the atomic bomb, a new hindsight respectability fell upon science fiction."

At the present, with rapid technological and social change being the order of the day, science fiction is enjoying a spectacular rebound from its long and often tainted history. Due to increased demand, most bookstores now stock a large number of science fiction titles and some even cater exclusively to such interests.

Science is now catching up with science fiction at a time when many people feel that we are being invaded by the twenty-first century. During the 1940's and 1950's the changes came at a regular pace, whereas now technological and social changes occur at a rate that may necessitate turning to science fiction as a shock absorber. Many seasoned readers of science fiction are more comfortable in today's world because they envision a future in which change will become the only real constant.

It is within this context that science fiction can be seen as a valuable tool for the reader. First, it prepares the reader for successful adaptation to change, for change is inevitable, although not always desirable. Second, it allows you to form a multitude of images of the future. Third, it can encourage you to take the necessary measures to reduce the negative impact of undesirable change and to promote those that are perceived as desirable.

Resistance to change is a deeply ingrained pattern in human existence. Traveling in foreign cultures, if we are not prepared, may be a miserable, alienating, and even dangerous endeavor; but, with proper forethought of what to expect, the contrast usually makes the experience rewarding and more than worth the effort. This applies to the reading, writing, and viewing of science fiction, which may be thought of as preparation for a voyage into the future—a travel agent for things to come.

When we plan to take a trip to an unfamiliar area, we cannot help but create certain mental images of what it may hold. If only one image is created and the mind becomes locked into it, the result may be disastrous for not living up to expectations. As we prepare for the future, it is therefore important to be equipped with multiple images of the future.

When you are in the market for an automobile, you do not usually accept the first one you look at. Time and effort is spent comparing the range of what is available, the options, the advantages, and the drawbacks of each model. The same careful consideration should be carried out when attempting to envision the future. The more visions that are contemplated, the better the final result. Science fiction allows us to envision more options and thus greater guidance in our voyage through the future.

The image of science fiction, even when it is catching up with science fact, suffers from a poor public image and is often the target of scorn. This is unfortunate, for as Asimov states:

> Science fiction is continually lumped under the heading "escape literature," and usually as the most extreme kind, in fact. Yet it does not escape into the "isn't" as most fiction does, or the "never was" as fantasy does, but into the "just possibly might be." It is an odd form of escape literature that worried its readers with atom bombs, overpopulation, bacterial warfare, trips to the moon, and other phenomena decades before the rest of the world had to take up the problems . . . No, no, if science fictions escapes, it is an escape into reality.*

In the last quarter of the twentieth century, science fiction is finally being recognized for its attributes and its role in futures studies. Arthur C. Clarke, who envisioned the communications satellite three decades before its development and who is the author of fifty books, many of them science fiction, has served as a consultant for industry.

---

*"Is Anyone There?" *The Futurist.* Vol. III (April 1969)

"In one bull session with Clarke," reports a business executive, "we get more ideas than many companies get from two years of management meeting." One of the reasons a corporation may seek help is because its management has been doing the same things with the same attitudes for too long without objective self-examination. Futuristic consultants, conscious of the necessity for adapting to change, are making valuable contributions to business and government.

Science fiction may be playing a multiple role by helping us adapt to change, facilitating the formulation of multiple images of the future, and encouraging desirable change while discouraging that which is deemed less desirable.

Utopia and Dystopia

Originating in ancient Greece, the word "utopia" literally means "noplace" and is defined as an ideal society especially in laws, government, and social conditions. A utopian is one who proposes or advocates utopian schemes. While most people are not true utopians, the study of the concept has been carried out for thousands of years. History reveals that many progressive ideas are debated for generations before they are brought into common practice. Such ideas as social security, parliamentary democracy, universal suffrage, and full employment, all now generally accepted, originated centuries ago in utopian images of the future. Oscar Wilde once said, "Progress is the realization of Utopias."

The first task of utopian thought, literature, or planning is to reflect the contemporary generation. The second is to reflect a counter-image of a possible future. As with science-fiction, the utopian image can help us imagine alternative futures and gauge our progress according to what we perceive as ideal. The Dutch futurist Fred Polak states in *The Image of the Future* that "All the art of social engineering could not place one stone upon another in the social edifice if the broad outlines of the system as an idea had not been projected long before, and if the seeds of the motivating ideals had not early been sowed in the hearts of men."

There are few words that have as many meanings for different people as "utopia." It would be impossible to describe a society in which everyone would be happy. Most would agree on such ends as security, prosperity, and peace; but a discussion of the means to these ends would result in disagreement and lack of consensus. This must not limit us though, for the realization that a utopia need not be perfect in all respects can free us to consider a plurality of utopias offering each individual a choice of living arrangements.

As outlined by Robert C. North in *The World That Could Be,* there are primarily three ways that alternative futures can be designed and utilized. One is the establishment of real-world organizations designed with the objective of accomplishing specific tasks within already existing societies. The second is formulating utopias on paper. The third involves utilizing computers, simulations, and forecasting techniques as a way of generating and testing alternative futures. Whichever method is used, they all draw upon utopian images of the future.

The opposite of utopia is anti-utopia or dystopia. The first major dystopian novel was Eugene Zamiatin's *We,* written three years after the Russian Revolution. *We* describes a nation in which peoples' names are numbers and whose God is "We" and whose devil is "I." During a period of social chaos, lobotomies are performed on the revolutionaries, including the narrator, whose last words are "Reason must prevail."

We, not widely read immediately after its publication, did eventually give rise to an outpouring of dystopian novels. In 1932 Aldous Huxley wrote the famous *Brave New World.* Equally well known is George Orwell's *1984,* written in 1949.

Orwell's dystopia offers a gripping vision of a thought-controlled, totalitarian world that has haunted the Western world for thirty years. More recent works, including Kurt Vonnegut's *Player Piano* and Anthony Burgess' *A Clockwork Orange*, share some of the main themes of dystopian literature—control, manipulation, conformity, violence, and a general return to barbarism.

Questions for Discussion

1. Do we seem closer to the future than to the past?
2. How do people cope with future shock?
3. What are some examples of obsolescence?
4. Is the generation gap wider than in previous ages? If so, why?
5. Are human beings really adaptable?
6. What traditions or institutions from the past would you like to see preserved in the future?
7. Do you find moving to another locality easy and exciting or upsetting and unsettling?
8. In *The Meaning of the Twentieth Century*, Kenneth Boulding states, "If all environments were stable, the well-adapted would simply take over the earth and the evolutionary process would stop. In a period of environmental change, however, it is the adaptable not the well-adpated who survive." Do you agree?
9. Are humans resistant to change?
10. Do you believe in the idea of steady and irreversible growth in human capabilities?
11. Do you think humankind can control its destiny?
12. Do you long for the Good Old Days?
13. Why is science fiction so popular today?
14. Do you agree with H.G. Wells' statement that "We are in a race between education and catastrophe?"
15. Is science now catching up with fiction?

16. Why is it important to develop multiple images of the future?

17. Do you agree with Isaac Asimov that science fiction is "an escape into reality"?

18. Why are corporations now hiring science fiction writers and futurists as consultants?

19. Are utopians escapists who are wasting their time?

20. What might Oscar Wilde have meant when he stated "Progress is the realization of Utopias?"

21. What does utopia mean to you? Dystopia?

22. What are some utopian elements in the world today? Dystopian elements?

23. What examples could be applied to the seven change factors?

24. What examples would tend to support Harman's advance indicators of change? What examples would refute them?

25. Do you accept the signs that may indicate a trend toward a challenge of legitimacy? If these trends are accepted as valid, are they desirable?

Activities

1. Design a possible future by writing a science fiction story.

2. Design a world not like Earth and describe life on it.

3. Design a utopia. A dystopia.

4. Study a science fiction novel, isolating the technological innovations and the social ideas.

5. If you have traveled, explain any cultural shock you may have experienced. How did you deal with it?

6. Look through magazines, newspapers, etc., for at least one example of each of the seven change factors.

7. Collect data and relate personal experiences of Harman's signs indicating a trend toward legitimacy challenge.

Primary Sources

Asimov, Isaac. "Is Anyone There?" *The Futurist,* Vol. III (April 1969).

Brentnor, Reginald, ed. *Science Fiction, Today and Tomorrow: A Discursive Symposium.* New York: Norton, 1978.

Cornish, Edward. *The Study of the Future: An Introduction to the Art and Science of Understanding and Shaping Tomorrow's World.* Washington: World Future Society, 1977.

Dunstar, Maryjane, and Garlan, Patricia W. *Worlds in the Making: Probes for Students of the Future.* Englewood Cliffs, N.J.: Prentice-Hall, 1970.

Fabun, Don. *Dimensions of Change.* Beverly Hills: Glencoe Press, 1971.

Harman, Willis W. *An Incomplete Guide to the Future.* San Francisco: San Francisco Book Co., 1976.

Negrin, Su. *Begin at Start: Some Thoughts on Personal Liberation and World Change.* Washington, N.J.: times Change Press, 1972.

North, Robert C. *The World that Could Be.* New York: Norton, 1978.

Polak, Fred. *The Image of the Future.* New York: Elsevier Scientific Publishing Co., 1973.

Toffler, Alvin. *Future Shock.* New York: Random House, 1970.

Toffler, Alvin. *Learning for Tomorrow: The Role of the Future in Education.* New York: Vintage Books, 1974.

Preview

All of us are forecasters of a sort, but much of our forecasting is so routine we are not always aware of the fact that we are engaged in it. From the time we get up our day is, at least to some extent, planned ahead of time based upon what we expect to happen or the many alternatives we realize may occur. A student, prior to taking an exam, attempts to visualize the nature of it based on the knowledge at hand and past experience. Before embarking on a vacation or business trip, people plan ahead knowing that neglecting to do so may result in disappointment if not personal disaster. These examples involve a constant series of exercises in futuristics aimed at helping us decide the best course of action.

It was not until the twentieth century that much thinking was devoted to the formulation of systematic methods of exploring the future, and even today there is debate as to whether forecasting is an art or a science. Many of the newer methods are strictly oriented toward forecasting but most can also be used for generating ideas, goal-setting, decision-making, and planning. All are now deeply woven into the fabric of our civilization as indicated by the fact that more than half of the 500 largest American corporations have established long-range planning programs.

The necessity of knowing where we are heading is the primary driving force in the expansion of the use and development of forecasting techniques. No matter how questionable our ability to forecast is, we must have some basis for making decisions for dealing with the future, particularly as we recognize the growing interdependence of civilization, of which changes in one sector affect many others. Furthermore, societal complexity is continually breeding more statistics giving us more data to work with. Finally, more sophisticated computerization is producing better forecasts, often at lower costs.

There are over 150 idea generating and forecasting techniques but the ones dealt with here are the most common and the most versatile, and none require extensive data computers or funding. What is required is an appreciation of the old Chinese proverb, "He who uses crystal ball may end up eating glass."

CHAPTER 2

TECHNIQUES

Six Principles Underlying Futures Research

Social systems, like living organisms, are usually highly complex and interdependent. Their behavior and evolution are the result of multitudes of different thoughts and actions operating in a dynamic mode of constant change. There are, however, a few ways in which the behavior of these systems are dependable and predictable. Futures research is, to a considerable extent, based on various combinations of principles that seem to characterize most social systems. Willis W. Harmon has outlined the following six principles underlying futures research:

1. *Continuity.* Societies tend to exhibit continuity, changing smoothly and usually not in discontinuous jumps. The principle of continuity is the foundation of most projections of trends and cycles. Example: The American Civil War did little to alter the traditional culture, social roles, and institutional framework of the past.

2. *Self-consistency.* Social systems tend to be internally self-consistent. The actions of one sector of society does not usually contradict that of another. Example: basic research is not likely to flourish when the economy is depressed.

3. *Similarities among social systems.* Although societal differences exist, similarities in human nature generally assure that the system will exhibit certain similarities. Example: the political structures of many developing nations tend to follow in stages similar to developed nations.

4. *Cause-effect relationships.* Generally accepted correlations usually imply cause and effect relations. Example: if scarcities occur, prices will rise.

5. *Holistic trending.* Social systems tend to function like

integrated wholes. Holistic, derived from the Greek word *holos,* means whole or complete rather than a portion of the system. Social systems must be perceived in holistic terms rather than focusing on a portion of the system.

6. *Goal seeking.* Although not necessarily declared, most societies have goals just the same as most individuals do. Example: Individual goals usually consist of a decent standard of living, good health, happy family life, a good job, etc. Similarly, societal goals typically include peace, economic stability, efficient government, competent leadership, law and order, etc.

There are few distinct ways that social systems are dependable but these six principles, if used cautiously, can be used as bases for different modes of futures studies.

Methods of Scientific Prediction

Social scientist Burnham Beckwith, author of *The Next 500 Years,* lists at the outset twelve ways to predict social trends.

1. Obtain data on continuing past trends and project them into the future.

2. Observe and determine public and expert opinion. Nearly all significant changes in social systems are preceded by gradual growth of supportung trends in opinion.

3. Observe current differences in opinion; between experts and the general public. *Many* social reforms being advocated by experts, but not publicly approved at present, will eventually be adopted.

4. Study differences between advancing countries and advanced countries and assume that the advancing countries will steadily become like the advanced.

5. Study differences between efficient and inefficient societal organizations and then assume that the less efficient will gradually adopt policies similar to the more efficient.

6. Study the differences in the consumption habits of the rich and the poor in any country and then assume that as real

income rises more people will adopt the habits peculiar to the rich.

7. Study the differences in the consumption and life styles of the most intelligent (or best educated) and the least intelligent (or least educated) and then assume that over a long period more people will adopt the habits of the most intelligent or best educated.

8. Discover successful pioneer social reforms in advanced nations and assume that they will eventually be adopted by other advanced nations.

9. Study all distinctive old customs and institutions which are peculiar to a single area and not justified by geography and assume that nearly all will gradually be replaced by more universal ones.

10. Analyze major recent or prospective technological developements and anticipate their social consequences.

11. Read science fiction and utopian works, selecting the most plausible developments in them, and determine if they can be supported by any of the above methods.

12. Develop new forecasts based on the premise: Humankind is partly rational and partly hedonistic and will eventually adopt nearly all major social reforms which would enhance its welfare.

Beckwith believes that a new inter-disciplinary science of predicting social trends will emerge during the next century. He foresees substantial growth in this field with increased funding devoted to this type of research. Consequently, the twelve methods of scientific prediction should be improved and new ones added.

Brainstorming

The method of brainstorming is simple yet productive. The idea is to think first and criticize later. Often we need not look for a particular "right" answer as much as a creative new solution based on rigid facts or strong analysis. Brainstorming is based on the belief that often good ideas are built upon other ideas, regardless of whether the others were good or bad. If this is true, it would follow that the volume of ideas can be, at least initially, more important than the quality when creativity is being sought.

The process involves a small group of people who are the brainstormers and one or two others to record the ideas on a large pad or chalkboard. The ideas are called out as they are thought of regardless of how silly, stupid, or crazy they may sound, while the recorders write them down as fast as possible. During this phase, no one is to criticize any idea. Any critical judgment is reserved for the second half of the session which is evaluation. Each idea, taken one by one, is scrutinized and ways are made to creatively link or apply the ideas as well as eliminating those of little or no value.

Futures Wheel

The futures wheel (Fig.2-1) is a method of discovering positive and negative implications of either a trend or an innovation. The trend or innovation under study is written in the center circle. Single lines branching off it indicate first-order implications, double lines indicate second-order implications, etc. A first-order implication is what is thought to be one immediate result of the trend or innovation. A second-order implication is a result of the first implication. Electronic news being brought into the home is an innovation with a first order implication being the elimination of newspapers being delivered to your door. A result of that would be a reduction of newspaper trucks which represents a second-order implication.

Scenario

A scenario may be called an alternative history in that it is a fictionalized forecast written from the frame of reference of a

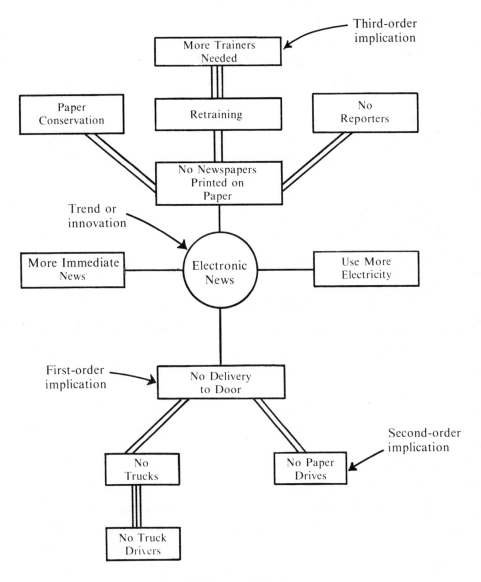

Fig. 2-1 Futures Wheel

future date. It involves looking back over the period between now and then as if it had already happened. A scenario is usually developed by

1. Researching information;
2. Choosing developments which might occur;
3. Imagining the sequence and range of developments that may occur.

When completed, a scenario should be examined to determine what assumptions are implicit in it and what assumptions are included which should not necessarily have been made. Branch points, which indicate times when specific alternatives were implemented or when new thoughts emerged, should be identifiable.

Scenarios may help explain what led to innovations, serve as summarizing tools, and assist in creating images of the future.

Cross-Impact Analysis

The cross-impact analysis provides a systematic method for examining the interactions among events, trends, or other data. The structure for carrying out such an analysis is called a cross-impact matrix and can be as simple or complex as necessary. The "cross-impact" part of the term refers to its ability to examine the impact of each variable on the others. The "matrix" part refers to the squire grid which is used to carry out the procedure.

For example, in Figure 2-2 the analyst records the impact of one of the alternatives listed in the left-hand margin with one of the general problems listed at the heads of the columns. One of the first interactions considered would be the effect of increased numbers of automobiles on urbanization. After the effects are recorded they can then be qualified using the following code:

Strong negative impact   (--)
Moderate negative impact   (—)

Fig. 2-2 Cross-Impact Matrix

	Transportation	Urbanization	Personal Health	Education	Government
Transportation a. More autos b. More public transit c. More walking d. Less traveling		a. b. c. d.	a. b. c. d.	a. b. c. d.	a. b. c. d.
Urbanization a. More sprawl b. Less growth c. Renewal d. Decay	a. b. c. d.		a. b. c. d.	a. b. c. d.	a. b. c. d.
Personal Health a. Greater health b. Less health c. Greater longevity d. More cost	a. b. c. d.	a. b. c. d.		a. b. c. d.	a. b. c. d.
Education a. More continued education b. More quality c. Less quality d. Fewer schools	a. b. c. d.	a. b. c. d.	a. b. c. d.		a. b. c. d.
Government a. More taxes b. More democracy c. Less democracy d. More bureaucracy	a. b. c. d.	a. b. c. d.	a. b. c. d.	a. b. c. d.	

No significant impact	(0)
Moderate positive impact	(+)
Strong positive impact	(++)

The four essential steps to completing a cross-impact analysis are the following:

1. Establishing the problem areas;
2. Listing the interactions;
3. Recording the reasons for each matrix entry;
4. Assigning a value to each impact.

Planners and decision makers often find the cross-impact analysis a useful tool and the applications to futures studies are numerous. More complex matrices are developed with the use of computers which can record the data faster and more systematically analyze the impacts.

Trend Analysis and Extrapolation

The simplest way to visualize the future is to assume that it will be exactly like the past. This is, for the most part, a highly erroneous assumption and will become increasingly so as time goes on. The next simplest way to shed light on the future is to assume that things will change in the same way they have in the past, that is to base your forecast on continuity. Continuity produces patterns or trends, and it is the analysis of these that form the basis of the most common method of forecasting.

Trend extrapolation is based on the premise that what has happened in the past can be utilized to forecast the future. The general direction of events (trends) are studied over a period of time and then projected into the future (extrapolated) using the pattern or trend as a base.

While it may seem logical and certainly convenient to assume that past changes will continue in the same direction and at the same rate as they did in the past, caution must be exercised when using trend extrapolation. Will the same factors necessarily continue into the future? A major drawback of trend extrapolation is that it fails to provide for trend reversals and major shifts. Unless there is a clear indication of a change many projections based on extrapolation are prone to error. For example, if your were a New Yorker living in the late 1800's, when horses were a major mode of transportation, it would be perfectly logical to assume that sometime in the future, as more and more people rode horses, the city would soon be up to its window sills in manure. This would have constituted a surprise-free forecast; the surprise being the invention and development of the automobile. A more contemporary example also involves the automobile. Up until only the last few years, historical trend analysis would indicate that people were driving cars with increasing horsepower. Extrapolation of this trend would indicate that people would be driving increasingly powerful cars in the future. Such is not the case—the surprise (shift, reversal) being the mass adoption of the small, economical car due to energy constraints.

A similar criticism of trend extrapolation is its tendency to show a steady line of progress into the future. Some futurists contend that this type of thinking is what got us into many of our present difficulties because trend extrapolation tends to encourage a "more of the same" attitude. Increasingly powerful weapons systems may be considered an example of this.

Why, with all the problems associated with trend extrapolating, do forecasters continue to use it? In the first place, trend extrapolation is responsible for most people's images of the future even though it may be based on intuitive feelings rather than rigorous research. Secondly, we are continually being presented with "predictions" from the media and we need to judge the reliability of these for ourselves. During inflationary times it is popular to project the price of commodities to a distant point in the future. The result is overwhelming but its actual validity must be questioned. Third, trend extrapolation can help us act to avoid trends which we may consider undesirable. Fourth, it often provides the methodological or conceptual basis for other, more complex tools. Fifth, it forces the analyst to learn more about the history of the particular subject being forecast. Lastly, trend extrapolation is relatively easy to execute, being one of the least complex and straightforward methods necessitating a minimal amount of data.

In order to capture the strengths and avoid the pitfalls of trend extrapolation the following questions should be asked of a trend being studied. The trend toward earlier retirement from employment will serve to clarify the use of these questions.

1. What are the natural limits of the trend? (Example: Is a five year old child likely to retire?)

2. What are the artificial limits to the trend? (Example: Is there a point when the economy may be unable to compensate for the trend?)

3. What is the demography of the trend? (Example: Is the trend concentrated in only certain segments of the population?)

4. what is the sociology of the trend? (Example: Is there a **point when institutions may intervene?**)

5. What is the psychology of the trend? (Example: Is there a point when the individual may no longer accept the trend?)

6. What specific technologies amplify or deamplify the trend? (Example: Will increased automation amplify the trend? Will medical technology which increases the life span deamplify the trend?)

By applying these questions to the trend the analyst is able to recognize forcing factors which either promote, retard, or in some way alter the trend.

32

Upon completion of the extrapolation process the trend may further be analyzed by applying these questions as outlined by Kim Quaile Hill.*

1. What will be the consequences if this trend continues unabated for X years?

2. What will be the consequences if this trend levels off or accelerates from its current rate of increase?

3. Which forces acting to maintain this trend are likely to remain constant and which are likely to change in the future?

4. If we wish to alter this trend in a particular direction, what determining variables might themselves be manipulated to do so.

Trend analysis and extrapolation is not only one of the oldest but also one of the most widely used methods for forecasting. Natural scientists, social scientists, urban planners, business forecasters, and many others in various fields find this approach to be the most basic, useful, and flexible tool available. If it is true that future problems have their roots in today's trends, the analysis of them can be powerful and productive if used with care and insight.

Delphi Technique

The word Delphi refers to the legendary site of the most revered oracle in ancient Greece. The powerful Apollo, master of Delphi, was known for his ability to foresee the future. His home, a beautiful temple near Athens, was built over a geologic fault through which fumes escaped. These fumes put intermediaries, women known as Pythia, into trances and their utterances were then interpreted by priests and then given to the petitioners.

Developed in the late 1950's, the Delphi technique attempts to identify developments that may occur in the future by rank-

---

*"Trend Extrapolation" Kim Quaile Hill, *Handbook of Futures Research,* edited by Jib Fowles. 1978. pg. 271

ing them according to probability, feasibility, and timing. It was designed to overcome the limitations in face-to-face conferences such as the prestige of a certain participant, the shyness of others, or "follow the leader" tendencies which often cause distortions in the final opinion of group conferences.

The technique is essentially a polling process consisting of the following steps:

1. The coordinator sends a series of questions to experts in the field who are willing to participate.

2. The same questions may be given to the experts a number of times, but each time they are informed of the results of the previous poll. The coordinator indicates what the average responses are and may ask those who offered extreme views to justify their positions. Their reasons are then given to the rest of the group.

3. The experts can revise their opinions but are also free to adhere to their original positions.

The credibility of the Delphi technique is seriously questioned for a number of reasons. They include the following:

● it tends to suppress extreme points of view in favor of achieving a consensus.

● the questions are often vague and subject to varying interpretations.

● it is difficult to define expertise. An expert may be very knowledgeable in one field but lack understanding in others outside of his or her specialization.

● there is always a certain percentage of those invited to participate who fail to respond. This may distort the findings.

The first significant Delphi forecasts were not made until the mid 1960's so they are only now beginning to be evaluated for accuracy. The results should aid in the development of necessary refinements in the technique.

Modeling, Simulation, Gaming

Modeling, simulation, and gaming are becoming increasingly popular as tools for educators, businesspersons, and government policymakers. All three tools make it easier to learn about something by being able to work with it in a manner more tangible than real life. They often provide the user greater flexibility, control, and simplicity by allowing easy manipulation of the different variables representing a real entity or process.

Automobile designers build models in order to run tests on them to determine how the real vehicle will respond. Medical schools use model "patients" made of artificial materials to train students. A model in which humans can actively participate becomes a simulation. Participants take on roles such as landlords in a city simulation or generals in a war simulation. When a simulation adds human motivation, often in competitive situations, it is called gaming.

A well structured model, simulation, or game that accurately represents a real situation facilitates the exploration of various future possibilities. As is often the case with other methods, the most sophisticated work of this sort is now being done in conjunction with computers based on mathematical data.

Decision Tree

A decision tree is a diagrammatic technique to map a route to a future goal. The goal can be personal, such as how to become a professional hockey player, or institutional, such as how to facilitate the use of solar energy.

Figure 2-3 illustrates the guidelines for using a decision tree.

Figure 2-4 illustrates a completed decision tree with the goal of providing 80 percent of heat and electricity by solar panels on all Oregon homes by 1990.

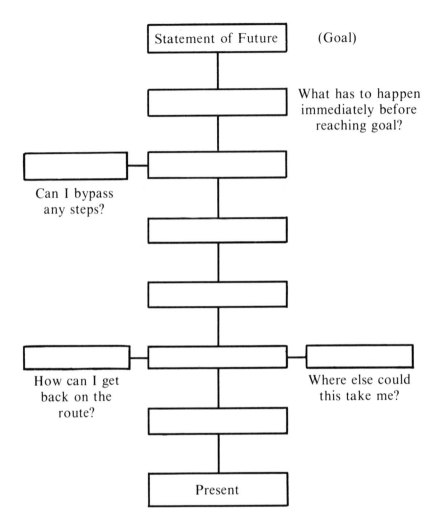

Fig. 2-3 Decision Tree

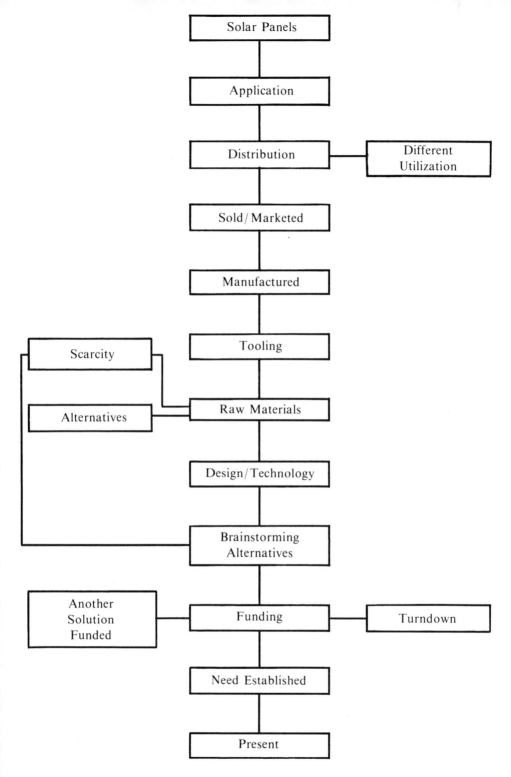

Fig. 2-4 Completed Decision Tree

By using a simple structure such as the decision tree the planner can identify potential dangers and opportunities, assess alternative policies and actions, and increase the degree of choice.

Questions for Discussion

1. Is forecasting an art or a science?

2. Why do corporations have long-range planning programs?

3. What are some surprises that may have altered forecasts in the past? What are some that may alter our future?

Activities

1. Brainstorm the following:
   a. What a time capsule should contain.
   b. How to get people to stop smoking cigarettes.
   c. How many different ways to get to work.
   d. How many ways a person could catch fish.

2. Complete a futures wheel for the following:
   a. The increased use of bicycles.
   b. Underground structures.
   c. More people eating away from home.

3. Write a scenario based on the following:
   a. The day grass reappeared.
   b. When all national boundaries were abolished.
   c. When only the rich could afford to drive automobiles.

4. Conduct a Delphi poll. For example, the following events may occur by 1993. Rank them according to probability and desirability.

   a. Funding for United States space exploration will be terminated.

   b. A female will be president.

   c. A long-term gasoline rationing plan will be established in the United States.

d. Only one out of ten people will live in communities of less than 100,000.

e. Average retirement age will be fifty.

5. Formulate a goal and diagram a decision tree to facilitate the achievement of it.

Primary Sources

Beckwith, Burnham P. *The Next 500 Years: Scientific Predictions of Major Trends.* New York: Exposition Press, 1967.

Dickson, Paul. *The Future File: A Guide for People with One foot in the 21st Century.* New York: Rawson Associates Publishing, Inc., 1977.

Harman, Willis W. *An Incomplete Guide to the Future.* San Francisco: San Francisco Book Co., 1976.

Kauffman, Draper L. *Teaching the Future: A Guide to Future-Oriented Education.* Palm Springs, Calif.: ETC Publications, 1976.

Preview

By the time you finish this sentence, seven babies will be born and almost four people will die on Earth. At the present rate of growth, the world will be inhabited by twice as many people in the year 2023 as it is today. A child born today and living to a mature age may experience a world of four times as many people. We are currently increasing our population by almost seventy million persons per year, which is the equivalent of adding the population of California, New York, Pennsylvania, Texas, and Illinois to the world each year.

To grasp a fundamental understanding of human population dynamics, with all the available statistics and models available, can be a frustrating experience. Endless analogies can be made, but the concept of doubling time may best illustrate the issue. Doubling time is the time necessary for a population to double in size. To relate doubling time to population, we must first determine the growth rate of the population. This is done by subtracting the death rate from the birth rate. As long as the birth rate is greater than the death rate, there will be growth. At the present time the global rate of increase is approximately 1.7 percent, which does not sound alarming. It does become alarming, though, when this annual percent of increase is correlated with doubling time. If the 1.7 percent rate of increase remains constant, the population will double in forty-one years.

$$\text{Approximate doubling time (years)} = \frac{70}{\% \text{ growth}} = \frac{70}{1.7} = 41 \text{ years}$$

The birth rate and death rate are so out of balance that the world population is increasing by 200,000 each day, or 73 million each year. If a person spent one second greeting each new inhabitant added during the past year, working twenty-four hours a day, it would take two and one-half years to greet them, and during that time 183 million more people would have been born, putting you six and one-half years behind in your cordiality.

Demographic considerations now play a large role in the formulation of social and economic policy, due largely to a widespread public awareness. Such considerations will play a larger role as we continue to more fully appreciate the powerful interplay between the dynamics of population and alternative futures.

CHAPTER 3

POPULATION

Age Distribution

During the next twenty years, most couples, at least in the United States, will probably have fewer children; but in spite of this the birth rate may rise. Why might this occur? The answer lies in the age structure or age distribution of the population — the percentage of persons at each age level of a population.

With the conclusion of World War II and the soldiers returning home, the United States experienced a baby boom which prevailed from 1947 to 1957. Women born in 1947 entered their peak reproductive years (20-29 years of age) in 1967 and remained there until 1977, while those born in 1957 entered this phase in 1977 and will remain there until 1987. The postwar baby boom has become the potential "mother boom" of the 1970 and 1980s. Dramatic increases in population growth thus affect society as it moves through an entire generation. Thus, even though many American couples are having fewer children, our population will rise substantially during the 1980s merely because there are more women who can have babies.

Age structure diagrams which plot the percentages of the total population in three age categories are useful in determining whether a population might expand, decline, or remain stationary. The categories are preproductive (ages 0-14), reproductive (ages 15 to 44), with prime reproductive ages 20-29), and post-productive (ages 45 to 70). A rapidly expanding population will have a very broad base with a great number of persons in the prime reproductive ages   approaching it.

About 37 percent of the world population is now under fifteen years of age, with about 42 percent living in the developing nations (Latin America, Africa, and Asia minus Japan) and about 28 percent in developed nations (the U.S. and Canada, Europe, the U.S.S.R., Japan, Australia, and New Zealand). These young people form the broad base of the age structure and represent a potential population explosion in the future.

Fertility Rate

Directly related to age distribution is the fertility rate. This rate — the number of births per one thousand women 15-44 years of age — in the world today is 4.7. If world population is to ever stop growing, this rate would have to fall to 2.5. Once this replacement level is reached, population would still grow for seventy to one hundred years before stabilizing because of the youthful age structure. Thus any plans to effectively control population growth must be made seventy to one hundred years before he goal will be reached.

There are clear signs of a fertility decline in some regions of the world. Most notably, China has experienced an estimated 20 percent drop in fertility during the last decade with the India reducing its approximately 10 percent.

Will world fertility continue to decline? The answer to this depends upon multiple factors which are continually interacting.

Marriage Age

If the average marriage age or the mother's average age at the birth of her first child rises, the fertility rate will normally drop. If the average marriage age is raised to twenty-four, the reproductive period is changed from 15 - 44 to 24 - 44, and the prime reproductive period is almost cut in half from 20 - 29 to 24 - 29. Such change will likely lead to a smaller number of children per family and accelerate trends toward a zero population growth.

Population Control

The population changes of modern times are a result of many factors, but basically they are a function of two opposite

trends: the declining growth rate in the developed countries and the acceleration of the rate in the developing countries. The demographic transition theory hold that societies tend to move through three stages: 1. High birth rate and high death rates, resulting in near stationary populations.

2. High birth rates but declining death rates, resulting in growing populations.

3. Low birth rates and low death rates, reestablishing near stationary populations.

A fundamental question is, why do the developed nations evolve to a reestablishment of near stationary populations? Who do the developed nations, all characterized by industrialization, complete the demographic transition where birth rates once again equal death rates? Some reasons for this are that children are too expensive to raise in an industrialized country, where they no longer provide cheap labor on the family farm because most of the people are not agriculturally oriented. Since the death rate is lower, the chances are greater that the child will live a longer life, reducing the incentive to have more children. Industrialized life is often crowded, and crowding lowers the birth rate; higher technology produces better contraceptives; and industrialized living requires education and generally education leads people to have fewer children.

In view of this many demographers look to industrialization to alter global population patterns. Others contend that even if this is assuredly the case, the process in unacceptably slow. There are, however, particular elements of development that are effective in reducing birthrates. These include the following:

● Reduction of infant and child mortality. When parents are reasonably assured that their children will live to adulthood, there is less incentive to have more babies.

● Expansion of basic education. Education tends to broaden one's choices and reduce resistance to family planning.

● Enhancing the status of women. Greater educational and career opportunities for women generally reduce fertility rates.

● Raising the age of marriage. Often linked with improving socioeconomic status, this factor has shown to significantly reduce birthrate.

To be globally aware, control of the world's population has come to the forefront as being one of the most urgent tasks of humankind. There is a definite trend toward greater world awareness of population problems.

The three basic approaches to reducing population growth are:

1. Voluntary population control.

2. Population control through economic incentives or disincentives.

3. Compulsory population control.

Whatever form these approaches may take, the single most important factor in a country's birth rate is the attitude of the people toward the regulation of birth. To deal with this we must first understand what motivates people to have or not to have children. Is it because women have been conditioned to believe that having children is the only way to find personal fulfillment? Is it because they love children? Is it to please the parents? Is it to provide old-age security? To save a marriage? To get attention? to satisfy the ego? The answers vary according to the individual and the culture, but of primary importance is that most people are only concerned with how many children they want and can afford without considering how many the community, nation, or world can afford.

A summary of various views of the population problem and how (or whether) to deal with it has been compiled by demographer Michael S. Teitelbaum. Positions against special population programs and policies include, but are not limited to:

● The view that favors rapid population growth to boost economic growth and an expanding labor supply, as well as to increase opportunities for economics of scale in small countries.

● Revolutionaries who may oppose population programs because they may alleviate the social and political injustices that often fuel revolutions.

● Those that view the motives of Western population control proponents with suspicion. Some regard population control as racist, exploitative, and genocidal to the nonwhite citizens of the developing nations.

● The belief that further improvements in agriculture and technology will permit accomodation of a much larger population that currently exists.

citizens of the developing nations.

● The belief that further improvements in agriculture and technology will permit accomodation of a much larger population that currently exists.

Positions supportive of population programs and policies include, but are not limited to:

- The conviction that the situation necessitates drastic action to restrain population growth.
- The belief that family planning programs are essential for reducing birth rates and that there is an unmet demand for birth control in the developing nations.
- The opinion that both population programs and social and economic development are needed.

These are not the only positions that we as individulas and societies have embraced, nor is any one of them likely to be held singulary by anyone.

We, as global citizens, should have begun long ago to analyze and take action to avert the population dilemma we find ourselves in today. But we did not, and time may be running out. Measures to control population that now seem excessive may one day be perceived as moderate and even welcome when the alternatives are considered.

Consequences of Overpopulation

What makes the population problem paramount and what are some of the manifestations of it? It has only been recently that many people have become acutely aware of the crisis, based not only on lack of food and space, but on the interrelated impact of many other variable all affected by population growth. Unprecedented stress is being placed on our ability to feed, clothe, educated, employ, and house the numbers of people that now occupy Earth. While these demands are becoming increasingly difficult to meet, we are also witnessing increases in population, environmentally induced illness, climatic change, overgrazing war, crowding, deforestation, and political conflict. The manifestations seem almost endless, but the logical conclusion is that each person added to the world's population puts at least some additional stress on the Earth.

induced illness, climatic change, overgrazing, war, crowding, deforestation, and political conflict. The manifestations seem almost endless, but the logical conclusion is that each person added to the world's population puts at least some additional stress on the Earth.

The problem with this conclusion is that it implies that we know what the optimim population ought to be — but we don't. At one extreme we are to be limited by the physical capacity of Earth itself and at the other extreme by the smallest group that can sustain itself. It is when we begin to consider the optimum level that we begin to debate the relationship between the quantity of people and the quality of life. Should the optimum level make possible a variety of lifestyles? Some individuals like close interaction and thrive on big city life. Others prefer a more solitary life. An optimum level will allow for both, recognizing the diversity of human needs.

Questions for Discussion

1. What feelings do you get when you feel crowded?

2. How are economic development and population related?

3. Is childbearing a right or a privilege?

4. How does age distribution affect society?

5. How could increased population lead to war?

6. Is American population growth a governmental problem or an individual problem, or no problem at all?

7. If population control is desired, should it be based on voluntary, economic incentive, or coercive means to achieve its goal?

Activities

1. Write a scenario of when the world reached twelve billion in population.

2. Write a pessimistic and / or optimistic scenario for the future population of the United States.

3. Using the Delphi technique, determine the optimum population for the world. Be prepared to back up your decision.

4. Complete a cross-impact analysis on the following suggested solution for overpopulation:

- Strict limits on the number of children a couple may have, with violators to be punished severely.

- Paying people not to have children.

- A negative income tax plan under which the fewer children a couple has the less tax they pay, with couple having more than two children subjected to very high tax rates.

- Free instruction in contraception available from government agencies.

- Sterilization of the poor.

- Reduced tax rates for those who adopt children.

6. Brainstorm causes of overpopulation.

7. Is birth control and family planning a form of genocide?

8. Complete a futures wheel on the implications of decreased population.

9. Brainstorm ways of educating people about birth control.

Primary Sources

Asimov, Isaac. *Earth: Our Crowded Spaceship.* Greenwich, Connecticut; Fawcett Publications, Inc., 1974.

Ehrlich, Paul R.; Enrlich, Anne H.; and Holdren, John P. *Ecoscience: Population, Resources, Environment,* W.H. Freeman and Co., San Francisco, CA 1977.

Jacobson, Willard J. *Population Education: A Knowledge Base,* Teachers College Press, Columbia University, 1979.

Miller, George Tyler. *Living in the Environment.* Belmont, CA: Wadsworth Publishing Co., 1975.

van der Tak, Jean; Haub, Carl; and Murphy, Elaine. "A New Look at the Population Problem," *The Futurist,* Vol. XIV, (April 1980)

Preview

"Energy," says the physicist James Clerk Maxwell, "is the go of things." The meaning of this was never greater than in 1973 when gasoline and other petroleum products became difficult to obtain and more costly. The American consumer was suddenly confronted with a powerful realization—energy and raw materials are not to be taken for granted.

CHAPTER 4

NATURAL RESOURCES/ENERGY

Consumption

Americans use more natural resources than any other nationality in the world. Each day the average individual uses the energy from about 13 pounds of coal, 3 gallons of oil, 297 cubic feet of natural gas, 3.7 kilowatt hours of hydroelectric power, and .7 kilowatts of nuclear power, or about four times more energy than our great-grandparents.

While energy and natural resource comsumption is already high, it will continue to grow at an alarming pace. Between 1900 and 1965 world consumption increased almost 600 percent, and it has been projected that it will increase another 450 percent by the year 2000.

Depletion

At the present rate of consumption, when will the world's resources become seriously depleted? The answer to this is complex, evasive, and highly controversial depending upon the data used, how it is used, and who uses it. Any projection, though, must be based on two major set of data. The first is the estimated potentially available supply at existing prices and levels of technology. The second is the estimated annual rate of consumption. Any forecast of when supply may run out or become scarce is a product of the assumptions we make based on this data.

M. King Hubbert has developed the concept of depletion curves to represent various alternatives for the use and supply of nonrenewable resources. Figure 4-1 represents three different depletion patterns for nonrenewable resources depending upon the supply, rate of usage, and pattern of

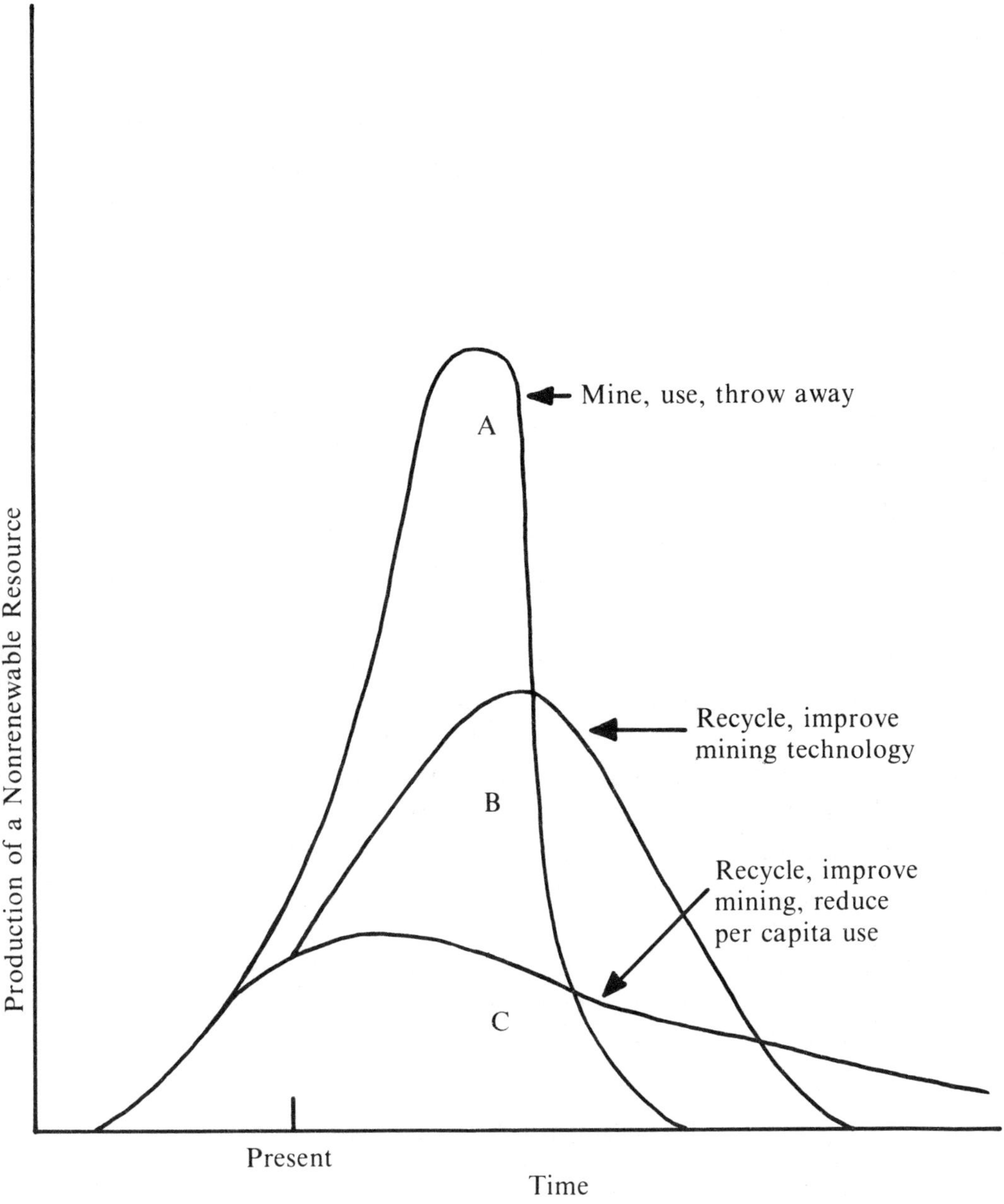

Fig. 4-1 Alternate depletion patterns for a nonrenewable resource. (Modified after Hubbert 1962 and Cloud 1971).

usage. Curve A represents our present system of mining, using, and throwing away a resource. Curve B utilizes recycling and improved mining technology, and curve C includes a reduction of per capita consumption. While this chart is very general, it does illustrate a useful approach to the study of natural resource depletion and signifies the importance of taking action now rather than some distant point in the future.

Importation

No modern industrialized nation is completely self-sufficient in the critical resources it uses. All the major world powers, except the U.S.S.R. and the People's Republic of China, import most of the resources on which their economy depends. The United States is importing more and more industrial raw materials; and, with usage increasing more than four percent per year, we will be forced to import even more. Within the next 30 years the gap between mineral production and demand may grow much wider.

There are 36 substances which are considered necessary to an industrialized nation. In 1970 the United States had to import 23 of them, and projections indicate that we will become even more dependent on imports in the future.

Why is this important? In a nation that is as heavily dependent upon foreign resources as the United States is, any disruption of trade may result in political and economic instability which may threaten international peace. In the past, wars have begun over trade disputes, and in this nuclear age potential conflict becomes even more frightening.

Minerals from the Sea

As mineral resources become increasingly scarce, scientists have begun investigating the oceans in the hope of finding untapped reserves. The seawater itself, sediments and deposits on the continental shelf, and sediments and nodules on the deep ocean floor are currently being studied.

Only magnesium, bromine, and table salt are abundant enough in seawater to make extraction profitable with present technology. Other minerals are present but are too dispersed to warrant extraction.

Offshore sites already produce oil, sand and gravel, and various minerals. About 17 percent of all oil and six percent of all natural gas comes from offshore wells, and this is expected to increase significantly. Ecological considerations remain as one of the main restrictions as oil leaks and spills are detrimental to the environment as is extensive dredging and mining.

Mining the deep ocean floor for minerals is seen as a source of hope by some scientists, but they may be overly optimistic. Manganese nodules, the size of potatoes, contain manganese, iron, and small amounts of copper, nickel, and cobalt; but they are unevenly distributed on the seabeds and only a few areas have nodules with high enough metallic content to make mining economically feasible. If the mining of these nodules is seen as profitable, juristictional disputes are going to increasingly threaten relations between the developed and developing nations. The developing nations would like any mining that is done in international waters to be conducted through the United Nations, whereas, the developed nations would like to pursue their mining plans uninhibited. Any such exploitation of the common heritage of humankind will certainly lead to resentment by the developing nations.

Conservation and Recycling

Until recently energy in the United States was taken for granted and this attitude, being as short-sighted as it was, has resulted in the squandering of vast amounts of nonrenewable resources. For decades energy was quite inexpensive to consume and the result has been waste. Consumption has long been synonymous with a high standard of living and a strong national economy. Given this heritage it is easy to understand why many may view energy conservation as threatening to their way of life as it seems to imply curtailment, rationing, and unemployment. Actually, it is more probable that such will result if we do not undertake a serious conservation effort now.

In the near term, conservation could do more than any of the conventional sources to help us adjust to a resource scarce environment. If the United States were to make a rigorous commitment to conservation, it may consume 30 to 40 percent less energy than it now does, and still enjoy the same or an even higher standard of living. No major technological breakthroughs are needed, only modest adjustments in the way we live. Ephemeralization—the process of doing more with less will be a powerful force in the decades ahead.

Conservation is a broad term but it can be thought of as a process of prolonging the useful life of resources over time. Seen in this respect, energy and resource conservation is the cheapest, safest, most productive alternative readily available in large amounts. Again, the real challenge is not to do it, but rather the confidence that it can be done.

An important element of energy resource conservation is recycling. While we spend billions of dollars to subsidize extractive methods to get the resources out of the ground as fast as possible, we fail to substantially subsidize secondary industries based on recovering and reusing these resources. It takes an aluminum can, by natural processes, 500 years to deteriorate, a plastic bag 240 years, and a glass bottle takes at least a million years to break down. The United States annually consumes about 190 million tons of metals, paper, glass, rubber, and textiles. Of this only about one-fourth is obtained from resource recovery operations.

If we are to reduce the impact of scarcities and pollution, more national planning is needed; industry must produce more durable and easily repairable goods; and perhaps most importantly, a while new public awareness and attitude must emerge. We must become a "recycle society" in which virtually all materials are reused indefinitely. This will be difficult for a society that has grown used to living in an era of conspicuous consumption and waste. For too many years our society and economic system has fostered the notion that "more in better." Samuel Hale, Jr., who at the age of 29 was appointed deputy assistant administrator for Solid Waste Management Programs of the Environmental Protection Agency, believes that, "We must move as quickly as we can toward a system, as well as a concept, of resource use that takes fully into account the undeniable fact that we cannot forever use the Earth as if it were a disposable commodity easily replaced tomorrow."

Environmental Considerations

Whenever energy is used there is an environmental impact so there is no environmentally neutral energy system. The use of energy permeates every level of the environmental crisis and is directly or indirectly responsible for most of our pollution. Whenever we turn on a light or start a car we contribute to the disruption of land, solid waste, and air and/or water pollution.

In the future, conflict will intensify between meeting increasing demands and attempting to maintain a sustainable environment. Remedies are costly. Emission control devices on automobiles add to the price just as pollution reduction equipment for industries ultimately costs the consumer more. How to maintain a balance between our need for energy and our desire for a clean environment is one of our toughest questions and will continue to be for many years into the future.

Conventional Sources of Energy
Fossil Fuels

There are three basic fossil fuel resources: oil, natural gas, and coal. These fuels, accounting for about 95 percent of the United States' energy consumption, are considered nonrenewable because their creation is so slow compared to how fast we use them. This raises two important questions. First, how much is available and, secondly, how long will they last under various assumptions of future use?

It is important to realize that these resources will never be completely exhausted. Eventually after using the best and most concentrated supplies and that closest to the surface, we will be left with only that which is of low quality, scarce, or so deep that it would require more energy to extract them than could be recovered by using the fuel once we had it.

Oil - Almost half of the total energy used in the United States comes from oil. It is difficult to overdramatize the importance of oil as an energy source, both domestically and globally. Every day about 45 million barrels move from producer to consumer and it is estimated that in order to meet demand growth expectations by the end of the 1980s this must expand to 70 million barrels. Yet virtually all forecasts indicate that the level of domestic oil production has begun irreversible decline and that global production can be expected to begin its descent before the end of the century. Revival of U.S. oil production sufficient to meet future demand does not appear possible.

Petroleum is not only used for energy but is valuable as a petrochemical. This includes lubricants, plastics, and detergents. Judging by their increasing number and the amount of research that is being done, the chemical industry will demand a greater share of the petroleum output in the future.

Natural gas - Natural gas is a clean and convenient fuel for cooking and heating but there are high costs and severe engineering challenges to be overcome in getting it to the consumer. By the year 2000, natural gas production in the major consuming nations will probably decline with North American production reaching a plateau by then and starting to decline thereafter. Thus, both oil and natural gas, the nation's two leading energy sources, appear to have a somewhat limited long-term future.

Coal - For many years coal declined in use, due mainly to a stronger emphasis on oil and natural gas, but this trend will reverse as oil and gas reserves begin to diminish. Initially coal seems to be a logical replacement since reserves are quite abundant but the environmental degradation caused by its mining and consumption is considerable.

When coal is utilized, particularly by power companies for the generation of electricity, air pollution is a result. Many particles and gases are eventually returned to the Earth by rain. By then these substances have gone through a complex chemical process whereby they have been transformed into sulfuric and nitric acids. "Acid rain" is now recognized as a growing threat to many forms of life and contributes to the erosion of buildings. Plant pathologist Leon S. Dochinger of the United States Department of Agriculture has stated, "Acid rain is perhaps the most serious environmental dilemma of this century." Thus, while coal's prospects may, in some ways, look brighter than those of oil and gas, it cannot by itself redress the energy supply deficit.

Nuclear Energy

It was not until the Second World War that the potential of nuclear energy was generally recognized. At that time research was directed toward and resulted in explosive force, in the atomic bomb, but eventually methods of slowing and controlling the process were developed. Now this technology is offered as a means of providing energy and has come to be one of the most important, complex, and controversial issues of our times.

One of its chief proponents is Glenn T. Seaborg who served as Chairman of the Atomic Energy Commission until 1971. He is convinced that nuclear energy will become an essential source of energy in the future although it now provides only a small percentage of electrical energy in the United States. Peaceful use of the atom, according to Seaborg, will allow civilization to continue to prosper with the full-scale development of nuclear power plants called nuplexes in which nuclear energy would generate electricity and desalt seawater in huge agro-industrial plants.

Others are less optimistic and believe that decisions dealing with nuclear energy should be made only after more extensive research, debate, and public education. Increasing numbers of scientists agree with this based upon the belief that nuclear energy is potentially the most hazardous of all sources of energy.

Nuclear power, now beset with a multitude of problems will not, at least in this century, deliver as much energy as one expected, nor at the low price that was earlier projected. Nevertheless, the nuclear option will be one of the continuing energy policy issues of the 1980s and beyond as differing views of whether the risks of pursuing - or not pursuing - a nuclear future are debated.

Unconventional Sources of Energy
Solar Energy

One the dusty, neglected shelves in the storage rooms of the Smithsonian Institution in Washington, D.C., some very brilliant, long forgotten inventions are being rediscovered and studied. These inventions use the sun's energy; but only recently, with the emergence of the energy crisis, have they enjoyed any relenvancy. Using many of these old principles in conjunction with sophisticated technology, it is generally agreed that solar energy is among the most promising sources of energy for the future and will supply 10 to 30 percent of our domestic needs by the year 2000.

Heating and cooling - In portions of the world where fossil fuels are scarce, expensive, or both, as in Japan, Australia, and Israel, solar water heaters and cookers have been used for many years. Solar energy can be used on a larger scale to heat and cool homes and buildings. Using the greenhouse effect, energy collectors coated with a black heat-absorbing material are mounted on the roof. Water, which circulates through pipes in the collector, carries the heat into the building's heating system. The heat can be stored in water, rocks, or chemical substances in insulated tanks. A solar air conditioner works much like a gas refrigerator only solar energy is used as fuel.

Electricity from the sun - Large solar electrical power plants are being proposed but have not been refined to a degree that would warrant actual application. One method under study involves building large desert solar "farms" in California and Arizona to produce solar energy and desalinate water. Large matrices of pipes would absorb solar radiation and by using a gas flowing through the pipes, the heat would be transferred to steam boilers where it would be converted to electricity.

A different approach would be to utilize a satellite in geosynchronous orbit meaning that the satellite would travel at the same speed as the Earth rotates so that, looking at it from Earth, it would collect solar energy by using photovoltaic cells to convert the sunlight into electricity. A transmitter would then convert the electricity to microwave energy. These mircrowaves would be beamed to Earth and received by huge "rectennas" placed on the outskirts of large cities. Many questions must be answered before the first solar satellite is built. With present technology the cost would be enormous, but this will likely come down as methods of production are steamlined. Another question being raised is the possible effect of microwaves in highly concentrated forms being transmitted to Earth. Another basic problem is the assembly of the satellite because it would be so large that it would have to be constructed in space. The ability to do this lies somewhere in the future.

Despite criticism of high cost and skepticism about a centralized "technological fix" that has grown out of the nuclear experience, an energy device known as the power tower is receiving generous federal budget outlays. Using a field of remote-controlled mirrors, sunlight is focused on a boiler at the top of a large tower. Amid many uncertainties, proving commercial feasibility could take the rest of the century.

Wind energy - Windmills, once quite popular but having fallen victim to central power stations, are now being seriously studied once again. Since wind is really a form of solar energy, it is a renewable, long-term source.

Wind energy researcher Dr. William E. Heronemus contends that large-scale wind energy production is presently feasible. He calculates that a band of about three hundred thousand wind turbines from Texas to the Dakotas could supply half the electrical needs of the country. The heavily populated East coast could be provided with electricity from floating wind turbines in the Atlantic. These floating platforms would probably use the energy to electrolyze water to produce hydrogen gas to be shipped or piped to land.

Small windmills have been used in rural areas for many years to either pump water or generate electricity. Now, increased enthusiasm, better materials, and extensive wind data are improving their efficiency.

Until the technology for storing energy improves, the intermittent and unreliable wind will continue producing intermittent and unreliable power. Another disadvantage may be visual pollution. The image of thousands of wind turbines dotting the landscape is less than comforting to some people. More research also needs to be done to determine if a concentration of turbines would alter the migration of birds.

Solar energy might also be collected by taking advantage of the temperature differences between the surface of the ocean and the deeper waters. Warm water could vaporize propane at high pressure which could then be used to power a turbine and generate electricity. The propane could be cooled and reused by using the deeper, cooler waters. Other systems harness ocean waves and tides but the possibility, at least in this century, of deriving significant amounts of energy from the seas appears ot be very slim.

Biomass - Every year the world produces one hundred billion tons of standing vegetation, aquatic crops, forestry and agricultural residues, and animal wastes. These substances, all produced by the process of photosynthesis, are called biomass.

Decomposing biomass can be used to produce methane which is very similiar to natural gas and is an excellent fuel. It has been proposed that "energy farms" be established where crops would be grown to be used as fuel for power plants or "digesters" which would convert the biomass to methane. Since only about 30 percent of the Earth is land, experiments are being conducted to rest the viability of using biomass grown in the ocean and other bodies of water. In the future, algae and kelp may be grown and harvested to provide us with a renewable source of energy.

Solid waste, more commonly known as garbage, is increasing by enormous amounts and is being considered as a source of energy by converting it to synthetic fuels, thereby reducing the impact of these wastes while providing a renewable energy source. Solid waste can also be mixed with coal as is done in St. Louis to reduce trash and conserve coal. As appealing as this sounds, there is one important disadvantage. About half of all solid waste is water so, unless collecting processing are improved or a new breakthrough in technology emerges, solid waste will have no significant impact on overall energy production in the immediate future.

Geothermal Energy

As evidenced by volcanoes and hot springs, the interior of the Earth contains heat which is produced primarily by the decay of radioactive materials. This heat is a valuable source of energy and may exist in the form of steam, hot water, and hot rock. These different sources necessitate, using different techniques, both for extraction and conversion, if the heat is to be converted to electricity.

The estimates of the potential of geothermal energy for producing electricity vary tremendously, but most would agree that it could supply us with an important share of our needs by the end of the century. Within the United States, most of the potential fields are located in the West, but they exist on nearly all continents. There are some environmental factors but they are all considered to be of less magnitude and more easily solved than those of fossil fuels and nuclear power.

Questions for Discussion

1. Is the price of oil too high or too low?
2. Do we need all the energy we use?
3. How could energy consumption be reduced in the world, the United States, communities, homes, schools?
4. Is it right for some countries to consume more than their population share of the world's nonrenewable energy and natural resources?
5. How can the individual practice ephemeralization?
6. Should the price of energy be raised in order to conserve it?
7. Should gasoline be rationed?

Activities

1. Conduct a Delphi poll on how the Federal energy budget should be allocated.

2. Debate the statement made by Ralph Nader, "The reason we don't have solar energy is that the oil companies don't own the sun.

3. Write a scenario about when the United States became a "recycle society."

4. Write a scenario about when acid rains were common.

Primary Sources

Crawley, Gerald M. *Energy.* New York: The McMillan Co., 1975.

Ehrlich, Paul R. and Anne H. *The End of Affluence: A Blueprint for Your Future.* Rivercity, Mass.: Rivercity Press, 1975.

Miller, George Tyler. *Living in the Environment.* Belmont, CA.: Wadsworth Publishing Co., 1975.

Schurr, Same H.; Darmstadter, Joel; Perry, Harry; Ramsay, William; Russell, Milton. *Energy in Amercian's Future: The Choices Before Us.* Baltimore and London: The Johns Hopkins University Press, 1979.

Stobaugh, Robert and Yergin, Daniel, ed. *Energy Future,* New York: Ballantine books, 1980.

Wilson, Carrol L., *Energy: Global Prospects 1985-2000.* New York, St. Louis, San Francisco: McGraw-Hill Book Co., 1977.

Preview

A fundamental lesson of ecology is that everyone and everything on the planet is interconnected. The goal of ecology, then, is to find out how everything is connected in an effort to discover how human activities generate environmental impacts - that is, activities which tend ot degrade or enhance

63

nature's capacity to sustain itself. Unfortunately, some of the most prominent scholars are offering quick and simple cures by reducing our complex environmental problems to a single factor such as population, affluence, or the misuse of technology. But the causes and the cure are complex because of their interdependent operations.

In addition to the inherent complexity within nature, different nations and people have different perspectives on the issues. The industrial world concentrates on air and water pollution and the exploitation of land due to urban sprawl while the developing nations focus on hunger, health, and lack of water. For the industrialist, environmental protection means higher costs. For the economist it means differences in supply and demand. For the hunter it means fewer game. Whatever way one views the environment, there are certain questions which we must consider. How pure do we want our water and what are its effects? How much growth is necessary and what are its effects? The questions are many and must be answered by people from all cultures and perspectives. Many kinds of pollution cross national boundaries and raise the questions of who is responsible for the "public" environment. Who owns the air over a city? Who owns the river that runs through a city or another country? We often treat the environment as a "no-man's-land" and, since much of it belongs to no one individual, it is left to the discretion of each individual, how he or she will use it. Unfortunately, it too often becomes the receptacle for everyone's waste. If this continues, we may challenge our ecological system to the point where it is incapable of supporting a reasonable human society.

CHAPTER 5

ENVIRONMENT/ECOLOGY

Four Laws of Ecology

Ecology does not approach the high degree that other scientific disciplines have, such as physics or chemistry. It is a young science that lacks cohesive, simplifying generalizations; but there does exist an informal set of four "laws of ecology" established by Barry Commoner.

1. *Everything is connected to everything else.* Ecosystems are in a constant state of flux and under normal circumstances maintain the ability to compensate for change and remain relatively stable. But the ecological network may also act as an amplifier so that even a small disturbance may have a dramatic effect on other parts of the system which then affects the entire system. It is similar to driving an automobile. As the automobile is driven down the road, adjustments in the steering are always being made in order to keep it traveling in a straight line. If too much adjustment is necessary, for example a hole in the road, the automobile will go off the road. In the same sense, an ecosystem will collapse when an adjustment is made so wide of the balance point that the system can no longer compensate for it.

2. *Everything must go somewhere.* This is based on a law of physics—that matter is indestructible. Nothing ever "goes away"; it simply moves from one location to another, converting to different molecular states, and affecting all that it encounters.

3. *Nature knows best.* Any major change brought about by humankind in a natural system is likely to be detrimental to that system. While this is a bold statement and may not always be true, it is an accurate generalization.

4. *There is no such thing as a free lunch.* This phrase, borrowed from economics, encompasses the previous three laws. It implies that for every gain there is a loss or cost. The global ecosystem, being interconnected in a closed system, will not allow humankind to extract anything from it without being replaced in some form.

Ecological Complexity and Stability

Green plants, which are the basic energy source for all life on Earth, derive their necessary ingredients through the many nutrient cycles of the biosphere. These cycles all convert wastes into resources, using energy from the Sun. Since all life is dependent on these cycles, such as the oxygen, carbon, and nitrogen cycles, it is important that disruptions through pollution and other human activities be carefully examined.

Ecosystems are composed of food chains that are complex and interlocking because most consumers feed on several different organisms. This interlacing of biological food chains is nature's way of insuring against disruptions. If one type of organism is eliminated, whether plant or animal, the remaining organisms can survive on other kinds of plants or animals. If this were not the case, a change in one link of the food chain would have disastrous consequences for the entire ecosystem. Through this complexity, overall stability is attained. Ecological stability is the ability of an ecosystem to withstand disturbances and to return to the conditions that preceded the disturbance.

In modern times humankind has often been an enemy of such complexity and, therefore, a destabilizing force by taking such actions as clearing, planting, mining, dredging, fishing, and all other forms of modification. Agriculture is the act of replacing complex natural ecosystems with simpler ones based on one crop. Pesticides and fertilizers are then needed to stave off the collapse to which their biological simplicity makes them susceptible.

Air Pollution

The form of pollution that most people are aware of is air pollution. Those that live in or near large cities can see it, smell it, and feel its effects when it causes the eyes to water and the respiratory system to become irritated. According to the Public Health Service, over 43 million Americans live in 300 cities which are considered to have major air pollution problems. At times the amount of sunlight hitting New York City is reduced by about 25 percent and that reaching Chicago by approximately 40 percent.

Unfortunately, the problem is not limited to cities but affects the entire atmosphere of Earth. Air pollution has been detected in such places as the North Pole and other remote areas. This is because, contrary to popular belief, we do not live at the bottom of an infinite sea of air. Our usable air supply is only twelve miles thick, and therefore the ability to absorb pollution is limited. More than 777,000 metric tons of air pollutants are poured into the atmosphere each day from the United States alone. This means that for each individual 3.5 kilograms, or 7.4 pounds, of pollution is emitted.

Where does it come from and what is it composed of? The major contributors, in decreasing order, are:
1. Transportation.
2. Fuel combustion from power plants.
3. Industry.
4. Forest and agricultural fires.
5. Incineration of solid wastes.

Beyond being unsightly and causing watering of the eyes, what other medical ailments can be attributed to air pollution? Detailed studies indicate that bronchitis, emphysema, heart attacks, headaches, nausea, asthma, cancer, and cirrhosis can often be attributed to the air we breathe. It can also contribute to head colds and pneumonia. In short, air pollution kills; but since it does so slowly and unobtrusively, the resulting deaths are not usually recorded in public health statistics. The same may be said for the deterioration of entire crops and forests which are detrimentally affected but with little public awareness.

If present trends are allowed to continue, the problems will become increasingly severe. In Mexico City "The metropolitan area is condemned to death by pollution before the year 2000" according to Ramon Ojeda Mestre, president of the Academy of Ecological Law. "So far," he says, "we have been able to keep one step ahead of catastrophe."

Water Pollution and Availability

At the turn of the century, water pollution in the United States was primarily responsible for typhoid fever, cholera, dysentary, and other infectious diseases. For many parts of the world these ailments are still a leading cause of illness and death; but, in the industrialized countries, filtration and chlorination have largely eliminated them.

Now there is new cause for concern, for as we have become more industrialized, new and complex wastes are causing numerous water pollution problems. It is not just sewage and industrial waste. It is fertilizer and animal manure, oil spills, DDT and mercury poisoning, detergents, foul smelling and discolored drinking water, smelly beaches, sediments from land erosion, radioactive wastes, and heated water from power plants and factories.

While there are many aspects to the problem of water pollution, one which all of us are concerned with comes through our faucets. The water in many cities is unsafe to drink. Chlorination helps, but it is becoming evident that high content of organic matter in water can protect viruses from its effect. Infectious hepatitis is spreading at an alarming rate in the United States, and this is largely attributed to the "toilet-to-mouth pipeline" in many water systems lacking sufficient sewage treatment. As the population of many municipalities grows, new treatment plants can only be built through taxes which are needed for other services.

The history of water pollution control in the United States is similar to that of air pollution; generally, it is too little effort applied too late. Beginning in 1969 an emphasis has been put on providing money for municipal waste-treatment plants; and, while this is certainly needed, it is inadequate to solve the entire problem. An anology may illuminate the issue. If your roof was leaking, you would not call a plumber to put a drain on the floor. You would instead hire a roofer to detect what is causing the leak and stop the trouble at the source. In essence, more treatment plants can only be a short-term, temporary solution; the problem must be identified and corrected at the source.

Faced with tougher water pollution laws, a number of industries have begun injecting their wastes into deep underground wells. In 1972 there were 278 of these, and the number is growing by at least thirty wells per year. Although most of these wells are presumed safe there have been several serious mishaps. Wastes that were injected in Canada came up from the ground in Michigan. Again we see the danger of the concept of "out of sight, out of mind."

Nowhere is this concept more evident than in our relationship with the ocean. All the rivers and lakes of the world—along with their pollution from cities, sewers, and farmland—eventually empty into the sea. But the sea has no outlets. We naively believe that the ocean will absorb all the waste we pump into it while at the same time we look to the sea for much needed food and resources. This is occurring when only a third of the world is industrialized and when industrial capacity is doubling every fifteen to twenty years. We are only now beginning to appreciate its vulnerability and that "dilution is not solution to pollution."

Just as Americans are beginning to recognize the long-range implications of water pollution, we are now sensing an impending shortage of this precious resource. To speak of a water "shortage" really means that there are more uses and users than available supply can accomodate. In just a matter of decades underground reserves of water have been seriously depleted and some ecologists are projecting that by the year 2000 there will be parts of Nebraska where water supplies will be so depleted that farming may never return. The water crisis of the future may make our present energy crisis seem insignificant.

Solid Wastes

The magnitude of the solid waste disposal problem can best be illustrated by figures. Each year in the United States we must dispose of 55 billion cans, 26 billion bottles and jars, 65 billion bottle caps, and more than $500 million worth of other packaging materials. In addition to this, seven million automobiles are junked each year.

It is becoming universally recognized that conventional methods of dealing with the problem are inadequate. Many cities are facing a crisis as population increase produces greater wastes while simultaneously reducing the available land for dumping.

When available, and under the right conditions, sanitary landfills which are covered over are adequate but in many cases open dumps are more than just eyesores. If the wastes are incinerated, they contribute to air pollution; water filtering through it may cause groundwater supplies to become polluted; and they serve as breeding grounds for rats, cockroaches, and flies.

Although accurate projections are difficult to make, at our present rate of increase—about 5 percent per year—urban wastes could double or almost triple by the year 2000.

Noise Pollution

The noise of modern living is assaulting our ears and health at an intensity approaching the level of permanent hearing damage. Many people, particularly urban dwellers, listen to a daily chorus of garbage collectors, clanking pipes, television, stereo, children, garbage disposals, dishwashers, vacuum cleaners, jackhammers, heavy traffic, bulldozers, typewriters, lawn mowers, jets, and air conditioners.

It has been estimated that 15 percent of the people in the United States now have significant hearing loss and that this is increasing rapidly. Approximately five million people under the age of 18 have impaired hearing.

What are the effects of noise pollution besides hearing impairment? Noise pollution may be a factor in many stress-related diseases such as peptic ulcers and hypertension. Sudden noises automatically cause blood vessel constriction, dilation of the pupils, wincing, suspension of breath, and stomach spasms. Constriction of the blood vessels can be permanent and increased blood pressure can contribute to heart disease.

If loud noise continues to be almost a way of life in the United States, by the year 2000 almost no one over the age of ten will have normal hearing. Fortunately the problem is easier to solve than other forms of pollution.

Pesticides, Herbicides, and Biocides

Whereas air and water pollution created by various forms of human waste have existed for thousands of years, pollution by pesticides dates from the 1940's. Anyone born after World War II has been exposed to pesticide pollution since birth. There are indications that this generation may, in the future, be resentful of what its predecessors have done.

The term pesticide refers to any chemical substance used to reduce the population growth of particular species believed

71

responsible for certain plant and animal diseases, spoilage, or wastage. Pesticides include herbicides, used for the control of undesirable plants and weeds; insecticides, used for insect control; and biocides, general pesticides that may be used to kill all life. The purpose behind their application may be perfectly laudable, but recently major problems have arisen from the development and overuse of certain of these substances. The problems include the following:

1. Indestructible pesticides accumulating in the ecosystems of the world.

2. Increasing pest resistance to them.

3. Their potential danger to humans and organisms in general.

Desertification

As a result of the misuse of land, deserts are creeping outward in parts of Africa, Asia, Australia, and the Americas. "Desertification" has become a familiar term to describe the desert encroachment and land deterioration that is afflicting many areas of the world and sapping the lands' ability to sustain agriculture and human habitation.

While desert encroachment is sometimes dramatic and evokes images of desert sands relentlessly engulfing fertile land, it is more accurate to think in terms of the desert being pulled outward by human actions. These actions involve continual deforestation, farming without adequate renewal of the soil, and overgrazing. Jens Hogel, head of the United Nations desertification program, says that this problem must be solved within the next two decades or the cost of doing so will become prohibitive. On that same time scale, if present trends continue, the world stands to lose a third of its arable land to desert.

Climatic Change

It is generally agreed that human activities affect the weather, but that is where any agreement ends. Some scientists contend that we are slowly warming our atmosphere due, in part, to the burning of fossil fuels, Others believe the opposite and have attempted to prove that we are increasing the reflectivity of Earth to solar radiation and thereby reducing the absorption of heat, contributing to an overall cooling trend. The worst danger may be in activities which destroy the life-protecting ozone in the upper atmosphere which screens out most of the deadly ultra violet radiation from the sun.

A warming trend appears most probable as a result of burning fossil fuels. The carbon dioxide that is released acts somewhat like the glass in a greenhouse, letting through short-wave radiation from the sun but trapping the longer-wave radiation by which the Earth loses heat to the atmosphere. If this continues, and it appears it will, we can expect a global warming that will continue into the first half of the next century. What changes may occur in the wake of a significant change in global climate?

1. *World Food Production:* There will likely be changes in the patterns of precipitation. Some crop-growing regions may benefit, others may deteriorate. Variances in growing seasons could influence the frequency, severity, and geographic distribution of insect pests.

2. *Human Health and Disease:* Altered climatic patterns could dramatically effect the breeding conditions, growth rates, and biological diversity of insects that transmit tropical diseases.

3. *Population Redistribution:* Climatic stresses could have a severe impact on national and international migration patterns. The ominous possibility of a temperature induced rise in sea level, due to a melting of polar ice, would make any

previous migrations seem small in comparison. If the polar caps melt, the oceans will rise 25 feet, drastically changing the coastal lines nearly everwhere. Forecasters state, at present trends, polar cap melting likely will occur before 2050.

4. *Considerations of Global Fairness:* The developed nations may find it demanded of them to pay the costs of controlling carbon dioxide emissions and compensation for the problems that might result from a global warming. On the other hand, without being offered inexpensive fuel alternatives, the developing nations may consider a call for limiting the use of carbon fuels a roadblock to industrialization.

Ecological Ethics

Ecological concern and action will be ineffective and of little significance in the future unless we deal with the attitudes and values that have led to the current environmental deterioration. This crisis is a result of our attitudes toward nature, technology, and one another.

There are many causes of our enviornmental ills and no simple answers, but it all comes down to what we as individuals and members of society are willing to do. What then can an individual do? To begin:

1. *Become more aware of the environment.* Look around your home, neighborhood, city, and the world and compare what *is* with what could and should be.

2. *Become ecologically informed.* Ecologize your particular area of interest and share this knowledge with others.

3. *Alter your lifestyle.* Adopt a lifestyle, particularly based on less consumption, so as to be less a part of the problem and more a part of the solution.

4. *Avoid the idea that if you can't change the entire world quickly, then we won't change any of it.* Remember that everything starts with the individual. Begin at the individual level and work outward.

5. *Become politically involved.* Start or join a local environmental group and/or a national organization. Large-scale pollution and environmental disruptions are caused by some industries, municipalities, and big agriculture.

6. *Don't make people feel guilty.* Don't preach to people but instead inform them and work with them.

Questions for Discussion

1. What are you willing to sacrifice for a clean environment?

2. Who owns the air over a city? A river that flows into another country?

Activities

1. Write a scenario about the day automobiles were banned from the city.

2. Write a scenario about the day the water got "too thin to plow and too thick to drink."

3. Brainstorm how to reduce noise pollution.

4. Complete a futures wheel centering on increasing desertification.

5. Brainstorm ways of changing your lifestyle to become more ecologically sound.

6. Complete a cross-impact matrix analysis on various forms of pollution.

7. Write a scenario of an acceptable plan to the world community to prevent the complete melting of the polar ice caps.

Primary Sources

Commoner, Barry. *The Closing Circle: Nature, Man, and Technology.* New York: Knopf, 1971.

Cronkite, Walter. *Universe.* Television broadcast of August 4, 1981.

Ehrlich, Paul R. and Anne H. *Population, Resources, Environment: Issues in Human Ecology.* San Francisco: W.H. Freeman, 1972.

Ewald, William, ed. *Environment and Change: The Next Fifty Years.* Bloomington, Indiana: University Press, 1968.

Kellogg, William W.; Schware, Robert; and Friedman, Edward. "The Earth's Climate: We're Finally Doing Something about the Weather, But We Don't Know What." *The Futurist,* Vol. XIV, (Oct. 1980).

Miller, George Tyler, *Living in the Environment.* Belmont, CA.: Wadsworth Publishing Co., 1975.

Preview

Some two-thirds of humankind are presently hungry and malnourished while widespread food shortages continue to appear inevitable. Millions of people still do not have enough food to fully realize their potential as human beings. According to World Bank projections that were recently released, the number of people living in hopeless poverty will decline by the year 2000, but 600 million persons will still go to bed hungry every night of their lives. At the present time about 800 million people live in absolute poverty—about four times the number of people living in the United States.

This is a grim predicament, one that should strike at the conscience of every civilized man and woman. Former Chancellor Willy Brandt of West Germany stated before the United Nations General Assembly in 1973, "Morally it makes no difference whether a man is killed in war or is condemned to starve to death by the indifference of others." A challenge to this indifference was put forth by President Kennedy at the

First World Food Congress when he said, "We have the means, we have the capacity to eliminate hunger from the face of the earth in our lifetime. We need only the will."

CHAPTER 6

FOOD

History

The present food crisis became obvious during the 1972-1973 crop year when total world food production declined from the previous year by 1.6 percent. That may not sound alarming, but what made it serious was the distribution of crop failures. It was the first time in over 30 years that the total world food production had declined. A 3 percent decline in Southern Asian countries reduced gains in the developing world, the home of two-thirds of the world's people, to zero.

The situation became worse when disastrous weather hit Canada, Australia, and the Soviet Union, reducing production in the developed world. The Soviet Union, usually a grain exporter, was forced to import massive amounts of grain from the United States. As a result, the United States grain reserves feel to their lowest level in 20 years. The world reserve capabilities in relation to consumption needs fell far below any previous level since World War II, to the equivalent of only 26 days' worth of world consumption. In 1961 the reserves represented 95 days' worth of world consumption.

The problems were compounded in the 1973-1974 crop year by severe reductions in the Peruvian anchovy catch which put pressure on supplies of grains, such as soybeans, for protein supplements in livestock feed. The Arab boycott in late 1973 created higher prices for petroleum and chemical supplies. This raised the price of fuel for farm equipment, chemicals for fertilizer and pesticides, and transportation of farm products. During the same time a long drought in the sub-Saharan countries affected millions of people, and famine began to take its toll. The world became aware of starving people and entire societies breaking down. It is difficult to fully grasp the severity of the situation when one has never had to actually worry about starving or living a life of constant agony due to malnourishment.

Affluence Breeds Overconsumption

In the past years the world food problem was analyzed by comparing the rates of increase in food production with those of population growth. But now, in addition to increasing population, rising affluence is seen as a major new drain on the world's food resources. Thus there are now two important sources of growth in world food production.

The effect of rising incomes on the world demand for food can best be understood by examining its effect on requirements for cereals, which dominate the world food economy. The majority of the world's people depend upon the direct consumption of grain as their main diet with the average person living in a developing country consuming less than 400 pounds per year. However, by consuming grain indirectly—in the form of red meats, poultry, eggs, milk, cheese, and other animal products—a person can consume far more grain. In the United States and Canada per capita grain consumption is currently approaching one ton, or 2240 pounds, per year. Of this total only about 150 pounds is consumed directly in the form of bread, pastries, and breakfast cereals. By feeding grain to cattle and poultry for producing milk, eggs, and meat, the average American exerts five times more pressure, in terms of land, water, and fertilizer on basic agricultural grain reserves than do most people in lesser developed nations. Using scarce grain to fatten farm animals is an inefficient method of grain utilization. In addition, the rich countries use most of the world's catch of fish. In the United States about half of the fish harvest is used for pet and poultry food.

Throughout the world, per capita grain requirements, both direct and indirect, rise with income and it is thought by many that we could meet the food problem by simply reducing our consumption of meat, which we fatten on scarce grains , thus releasing that grain for feeding hungry people. But we are not likely to do so as long as we continue to believe that our "just reward" for being good citizens and working hard is to live many times as wealthy as the people in some of the world's poorer nations. If we are willing to accept a level of consumption that is only two or three times what is necessary for health and well-being, we can help solve the problem of hunger in the world.

Land

From the beginning of agriculture until about 1950 most of the increase in world food output came from expansion of the areas under cultivation. Since 1950, however, the major increases—about four-fifths of the current gains in output—are due to intensification of cultivation on existing land area. Just how much land is potentially available for agriculture? Total global surface includes about 197 million square miles, but only 57 million square miles is land—the remaining 140 million is water. Of that global land surface, only 10 percent is now suitable for agricultural purposes, and most of that is now under cultivation. Additional land could be brought into agricultural production, but it could take from 30 to 35 years and an investment of some $500 billion to bring this land to full productivity. Intensifying the problem is the steady decline of available farmland due to urbanization creating more and more highways, airports, housing, and other elements of modern society. According to Rural America, a nonprofit organization, the United States is losing two million acres of farmland each year to urban development, highways, recreational facilities, and other nonagricultural uses. California loses 375 acres of farmland to commercial development each day.

At a time when millions of people are starving, thousands of acres of fertile land are being paved to build new shopping centers and other "necessities" of life in affluent America. When are we going to realize that they quit making land a long time ago?

Water

One of the principle constraints on efforts to expand world food production in the years ahead may be lack of water. There are still large amounts of potentially productive land throughout the world that essentially only lacks water in order to be fertile. But many of the rivers suitable for damming and irrigation have already been developed. Future efforts to increase fresh-water supplies for agricultural purposes will focus increasingly on alternative techniques. The diversion of rivers, the artificial seeding of clouds or manipulation of rainfall patterns, which may increase the share of rain falling over moisture-deficient areas, could offer hope. The desalting of seawater has moved from the experimental stage and is now economically practical in limited areas. Inexpensive methods of desalting seawater and then using it for irrigation could literally make the deserts bloom. A different approach would be the development of crop strains that thrive on brackish water and thus do not require such clean water.

Haves/Have-Nots

In thinking about the global food problem, you must divide people of the world into two categories—the developed nations and the developing nations. In general, because of their low birth rates and advanced technology, the developed nations can either produce enough food for their people or can afford to import it. But the less developed nations are not yet making significant progress in population control and the result may increase the gap between the "haves" and the "have-nots." This development is politically and diplomatically very dangerous in a shrinking world. The poor countries may not be able to pay for food imports from the rich countries, although they desperately need it. What we must try to bring about is a rate of economic growth sufficient to allow the poorer nations to buy the additional food they will need. But it is questionable whether they will be able to achieve such rapid economic growth. On the other hand, if the rich countries transfer food on some sort of concessional basis, the imported food may depress their local price levels, inhibit their own agricultural production, and make them dependent on the rich nations for continued donations. However, if the poor countries continue to increase their population without additional economic growth and if the developed nations are unwilling to feed them, many people of the poor nations may be destined to malnutrition resulting in physical and mental weakness, lack of energy, vulnerability to disease, poor educational systems, slow progress in industrialization, and a good deal of social turmoil which may express itself in rioting, revolutions, civil wars, and wars between nations.

Geographic Shift

The world's major unrealized potential for expanding agricultural production is now concentrated in the developing nations. As resources become scarce, the comparative advantage in additional food production shifts toward those areas where conditions offer the highest returns. Today, an additional ton of fertilizer or gallon of fuel can produce an increase in food output far higher in the developing nation than in the developed ones. An additional pound of fertilizer may only return five additional pounds of grain in the industrialized nations; but in countries such as India, Indonesia, or Brazil, another pound can yield at least ten additional pounds of grain. It is unfortunate that in 1973, when fertilizer shortages emerged, the more advanced nations acted to restrict their fertilizer exports to the poor nations where it could have produced more food. The soil quality in Bangladesh is as good as in Japan, yet rice yields are only one-third of those attained in Japan. India has approximately the same area of crop land as the United States, yet it harvests only 100 million tons of grain while the United States harvests 250 million tons.

Lack of Purchasing Power

Traditionally, the world food situation has been a matter of calculating the projected demand for food against the technological potential for increasing the supply. It is possible to imagine a vast increase of world food output based on known reserves of land and water achieved by greater amounts of energy, fertilizer, and management techniques. There is little doubt that there is great opportunity for expanding food supplies, but this is not the real problem. The real issue is at what price we can bring the additional resources into use. We must consider the following factors:

1. Most good land in the world is already under cultivation.

2. With a few exceptions, the most desirable irrigation sites already have been developed.

3. Energy, and therefore fertilizer, will be more costly in the future than in the past.

4. In the more advanced countries, where yields are already high, further increases in production will be far more costly than those of the past.

In order to bring these additional reserves into use, the price of food must increase; but, unfortunately, recent food price rises have already far exceeded growth in income among millions of the world's poorest people. When people spend about 80 percent of their income on food, as much of humankind does, a rapid rise in the price of wheat or rice cannot be offset. Instead of merely paying more for necessary food, the increased price drives a subsistence diet below the survival level. This development reverses the long-term trend of improved nutrition, lengthening life expectancy and declining infant mortality in many of the poorer nations.

For many people in the world, an increase in the cost of food does not mean that they will have to reduce the number of movies they go to or the number of records they buy—it means they will have less food to eat.

Rural-Urban Migration/Mechanization

An increasing number of people in the developing world are moving from the rural area to the urban areas. There are at least three reasons why this is occurring. The first is that a large number of young people are reaching employable age and the second is the lack of opportunity in the countryside. These two factors encourage people to move to urban areas in hope of finding a job because farming no longer offers a decent livelihood. The third factor contributing to the rural-to-urban migration is the mechanization of farm production. Traditionally, mechanization has always been thought of as labor and thus contributes to unemployment. The unemployed farm worker is then often forced to seek work in the city, which may already be overcrowded. Nevertheless, with careful and long-range planning, mechanization may be implemented selectively so as to expand rural employment rather than diminish it. For example, when tractors are used in place of human labor, seedbed preparation can be hastened and three or four crops can be raised in a single year. The tractors reduce the labor required to prepare the seedbed, but increases the number of crops produced, creating more employment. The solution is to encourage selective mechanization and intensive cropping, both of which create jobs.

Intermediate Technology

During the last twenty years the developed nations have expended efforts to develop the technologies of the emerging nations, and the results have not always been satisfactory. The Green Revolution, a program initiated by the United States in the 1960's with the goal of helping to alleviate hunger in the poorer nations, soon discovered that it does little good to send expensive, complex farm machinery to a nation that lacks replacement parts, tools to repair the machinery, or the necessary capital to maintain it.

Most developing nations are capital-poor and manpower-rich and therefore can best be helped by providing them with the skills and knowledge needed to develop intermediate or appropriate technology—systems that require simple machines and hand tools rather than highly sophisticated technology. An example of using intermediate technology would be to replace wooden plows with steel ones because people in developing countries understand and adopt such changes more readily than trying to use a mechanized tractor which is totally alien to their experience.

It does little good and may even perpetuate the food crisis to send complex, expensive farm machinery to a nation that cannot afford replacement parts when it breaks down. It does, though, provide profits to the large manufacturing corporations that sell them the machinery.

The "Protectionist" Myth

It is believed by some that, if the rich countries help the poor countries, they will increase their agricultural output and eventually get into the world market and take away the rich nations' export market. Actually, past experience shows that when the agricultural output of a nation is increased, the people then become better off, their income rises, and they become good customers for the wealthier nations.

It would be, in the long-term, advantageous to have a more even distribution of wealth throughout the world for this would allow trade to flourish, benefitting buyers and sellers alike. A society that encourages short-term benefits rather than long-term objectives finds this difficult to perceive.

Triage

Triage is a term that came about during World War I. It is a system used in military medicine to assign priority to the wounded in times of mass casualties and limited medical facilities. The wounded are divided on the basis of three classifications:

1. Those so seriously wounded they cannot survive regardless of the treatment given them.

2. Those who can survive without treatment regardless of the pain they may be suffering.

3. Those who can be saved by immediate medical care.

The practice of triage is a horrible chore for the doctors who must classify the wounded in this manner, but many people believe that it is the only way to save the maximum number of lives. To spend valuable time with the less severly wounded or with the dying would mean that many of those who might have lived will die. It would be a misuse of the available medical help.

In applying triage to the world food situation, the developed nations would represent the medical staff while the hungry nations would represent the ones in need of medical attention.

Many experts refute this entire concept on the basis that it is possible to significantly help all nations, regardless of their condition, if only action is taken now.

The Big Farming Business

It is seen by many that as time goes on more and more food production is being taken out of the hands of the small farmers and increasingly being tied into a new class of local and international corporations. We see emerging a "global supermarket" brought about by these corporations growing food in one country and then selling it to a different country, resulting in local foods going less and less to local people. In the course of this transformation the hungry are being cut out of the production process. To be severed from the production process is to be cut out of consumption. How does this come about?

● *Some of the food goes to urban middle-income groups.* Hybrid seeds and other inputs increase yields, but if grown by a relatively few farmers who are not dependent upon the crop directly, it may be processed into sweetner for soft drinks for the urban middle and upper classes.

● *Some of it gets fed to livestock.* The Green Revolution is an effort to increase food productivity in the developing nations. In 1973, two-thirds of the Green Revolution rice in Columbia was going to feedlots and breweries. The poor cannot afford beef or liquor.

● *Some of it gets exported.* If a country imports agricultural inputs such as machinery, fertilizer, etc., it must export to earn money to pay for it. Despite the malnutrition of 80 percent of its rural population, Mexico in the late 1960's began to export its Green Revolution wheat. In addition, some of the additional inputs, which were intended to boost grain production, were used to raise carnations which were then exported. Poor people cannot eat carnations.

"Agribusiness," large corporations that produce food is sometimes seen as creating obstacles which prevent people from taking control of the production process and thus feeding themselves.

In order to protect their markets, developed nations sometimes deny developing nations the opportunity to produce more food by such practices as trade restrictions and pricing systems that undermine incentives to produce surpluses.

Hybrids

Research is being conducted which is producing hybrid strains of grain. Hybridization is the production of offspring from genetically different parents. A new grain called triticale is very high-yielding, very nutritious, and promises to be the most significant development in food grain since the discovery of corn over 400 years ago. The name triticale is derived from the scientific names for wheat (Triticum) and rye (Secale). This new grain also has the ability to withstand cold and has the ability to grow on infertile, sandy soils. With further breeding it holds promise of becoming resistant to wheat rust, a disease that lowers wheat production over much of the world. Due to these traits, triticale may enable farmers to grow grain on marginal land, that is, land that was formerly incapable of growing anything. This would, of course, significantly increase the world's food supply.

While hybridization offers hope of reducing world hunger, it is not without its problems. It would seem that all that is needed is to transfer the hybrid grain seed from the developed world to the developing world, but such automatic transference is rarely possible. In most cases the particular grain is not able to adapt to the peculiar conditions imposed by local soils and climate within the developing nations. Even if it were able to adapt to the new conditions, a disease or insect to which it was not resistant might attack it and destroy all or most of the crop.

Individual Efforts

Experiments are now being carried out by a number of individuals and organizations that offer the hope of easing the food crisis and also making one's life more meaningful. Sound ecological principles are being applied not only on the large scale but also at the level of the individual home. Relatively self-contained homes are now being heated by the sun, insulated with earth and sod, powered by the wind, sewage is composed, and food is grown in greenhouses. The houses make maximum use of energy techniques in cooking, ventilation, heating, and lighting.

Roof space, which may constitute one-third of the urban surface area, is now being utilized for growing vegetables and, in many eastern countries, even raising chickens. Unused land, owned by the county, is being used for neighborhood gardens, and in some areas the county offers gardening classes and water outlets.

Other possibilities also exist. One group in Washington, D.C., is experimenting with raising trout in basement tanks. Houses are being designed in which fruit trees are part of the decor; an occupant can pick a banana for breakfast without getting out of bed.

Given today's grim outlook on the world food situation, it may not be important that an urban greenhouse or a basement fish tank cannot overnight provide us with a solution to the problem, but the fact that they exist could provide a promise that tomorrow can be better. That idea alone could be an important contribution.

A Scenario

The research that is being done today is laying the foundation of the world we may be living in 25 or 30 years from now.

Let's assume that the most advanced methods of agriculture have reached the stage of practical application by then.

Advanced space satellites will be supplying intelligence for the farmers of tomorrow while they study reports in their air-conditioned offices. These satellites, equipped with sophisticated remote sensing instruments, are supplying the information needed to make key decisions. They are capable of detecting differences in soil, identifying different crops and trees, determining damage done by diseases, insects, and drought, and assessing crops in order to predict production. This information is gathered from all around the world and transmitted to computers for analysis and immediate application.

The various soils of the world have been inventoried and each crop is either grown on the soil best suited for it or on soil that has been chemically modified for maximum production. There is a running inventory of acreage and output of all crops and predictions are used to guide marketing and distribution to avoid waste and local shortages and surpluses.

If a control situation requests a check on the maturity of the North American wheat crop, a signal is sent to the spacecraft sensor and within minutes the results are in. If the grain in Oklahoma is ripening too fast and threatens to glut local markets, farmers in that area are then alerted to the situation, enabling them to manipulate artificial light and apply growth-regulating chemicals to slow the maturity.

Resolutions

There are three basic ways to help alleviate world hunger:

1. Increase food aid from the United States and other developed nations.

2. Increase food production in the developing nations.

3. Reduce the rate of population growth.

Obviously, some combination of these measures can be pursued, or perhaps all of them simultaneously.

Questions for Discussion

1. Do you agree or disagree that "Morally it makes no difference whether a man is killed in a war or is condemned to starve to death by the indifference of others"?

2. Do the wealthy nations have the moral right to consume in the manner that they do?

3. Should the concept of a triage be applied to the current world food situation?

4. How could a relatively self-contained home make one's life more meaningful?

5. Do you agree or disagree that we need only the will to eliminate hunger in our lifetime?

6. How realistic is the scenario presented? Is it desirable?

7. What combination of resolutions presented in the chapter should be pursued? Others?

Activities

1. Plan menus which reflect both good nutrition and wise use of resources.

2. Write an alternative scenario to that presented in the chapter.

3. Develop an overall program to cope with world food problem during the rest of the 20th century.

Primary Sources

Boerma, Addeke H. "Solving the World's Food Problem," *The Futurist,* vol. VIII (April 1974).

Brown, Lester R. "Global Food Insecurity," *the Futurist,* Vol. VIII (April 1974).

Brown, Lester R. *Our Daily Bread.* New York: Foreign Policy Association, Inc., 1975.

Brown, Lester R., with Eckholm, Erik R. *By Bread Alone.* New York: Praeger, 1974.

Humphrey, Hubert H. "Helping the World Solve It's Food Problems," *The Futurist,* Vol. IX (Dec. 1975).

Johnson, D. Gale. *The Struggle Against World Hunger.* New York: Foreign Policy Association, Inc., 1967.

Lappe, Frances Moore, and Collins, Joseph. "More Food Means More Hunger," *The Futurist,* Vol. XI (April 1977).

Mayer, Jean. "The Struggle for an Adequate World Diet," *The Futurist,* Vol. IX (Dec. 1975).

Molitor, Graham T. "The Coming World Struggle for Food," *The Futurist,* Vol. VIII (Aug. 1974).

Paarlberg, Don. "A World Food Policy That Can Succeed," *The Futurist,* Vol. IX (Dec. 1975).

Selim, Robert. "The 1980's: A Decade of Hunger?" *The Futurist,* Vol. XIV (April 1980).

Preview

Most of the energy used throughout history has been to move people and things from one place to another.

The average American family spends between 14 and 18 percent of its income on transportation. When the industrial sector is figured in, it reaches 20 percent, or one-fifth, of our Gross National Product. That is an expenditure of over $200 billion just to move ourselves and our goods.

Every large city is today faced with a transportation problem of staggering proportions, and it will probably become worse before any real solutions are implemented. In other areas of the world, increasing population will eventually bring about similar problems that the developed world now faces.

The first spectacular breakthrough in communications was the telegraph which introduced message transmission. This separated communication from transportation and introduced the age of rapid communications. Surveys have indicated that 44 percent of all adults in the United States knew of President Kennedy's assassination within 15 minutes, 62 percent within 30 minutes, 80 percent within 45 minutes, and 90 percent within an hour.

Humankind may be at the brink of what some have called

the Second Industrial Revolution. Others call it the Information Age, Post-Industrial Era, Cybernetic Era, or the Synergetic Age. Whatever label is chosen, recent advances in the storage, retrieval, processing, and distribution of information have already laid the foundation. This is creating an entirely different culture from what we've ever known before, and because communications is an important part of the web that holds society together, it has to effect the way we think of ourselves. Today's information technology has altered the attitudes of hundreds of millions of people who have only started to recognize the complexity of the role it will play in the future.

By the 1990's, information will be more accessible, more diverse in format, and will have a much greater impact on the economy than even today. By the year 2000, a typical American home will be equipped with a communications center developed through the convergence of computers, communication networks, and video technologies. As with most technologies, there are tradeoffs. Privacy may be jeopardized at both the personal and corporate level as it is easy to envision computer files bursting with information that could be used in devious ways. With this in mind, we must brace ourselves for both the wonder and anxiety that will surely accompany the emergence of a new informationalized era.

CHAPTER 7

TRANSPORTATION/COMMUICATION

The Automobile

An objective survey of the automobile, the dominant form of transportation in the developed world, may provide a starting point for a study of future transportation systems.

The following is a list of the disadvantages of the automobile:

● The internal combustion engine is the main source of air pollution in the United States and other advanced nations.

● The internal combustion engine requires tremendous amounts of fuel which is becoming increasingly scarce and costly.

● Every year in the United States, 55,000 people are killed and about two million are seriously injured in auto accidents.

● Cars take up a lot of space. About half of all the land in a typical business area is occupied by streets, sidewalks, and parking lots.

● Automobiles are expensive for the individual to buy and maintain. When all individual and societal costs are added up, the automobile costs about one dollar per mile to operate.

● Rush hour congestion contributes to lost time, wasted energy, and short tempers. In 1907, the average speed of horse drawn vehicles through New York City's streets was 11.5 miles per hour. In 1966 the average speed of motor vehicles (with the power of 200-300 horses) through the central business district was 8.5 miles per hour—or during midday crushes slower still.

Several measures have been proposed or are being carried out in order to reduce the negative impact of the automobile. Among them are:

94

● Having the work day begin at various times and then end at different times which helps eliminate rush hour congestion.

● Car pooling whereby more than one person occupies the car. Having the inside lane of the freeway during certain hours reserved for cars with two or more people.

● Special gas, parking, and pollution taxes with the money going into efforts to solve the problems.

● Establishment of areas within the city where no cars are allowed.

The advantages of the automobile include:

● It is usually available at all times.

● The automobile will go in any direction at almost any speed the driver desires.

● It doesn't have to stop and pick up others.

● It allows the driver privacy.

Since the automobile is the dominant form of transportation and many people are quite aware of its advantages and disadvantages, it would make sense to use it as a reference in designing new transportation systems. Transit planners would do well to keep in mind the most attractive features of the auto that have drawn the public to it. After all, no public transportation system is any good if no one uses it. The challenge is to create a safe, fast, convenient, and comfortable transportation system which will not degrade the environment to the degree that current systems do.

Railroad Travel

Often considered a thing of the past, the railroad may become a major form of transportation as it once was in the past. One new development that may help to bring this about is based on the idea that a single rail line can carry from five to twenty times as many passengers as a lane of highway.

The first automated rail transit line began operation in 1969. Lindenwold is a 14½-mile run connecting Philadelphia with several bordering New Jersey communities. Only one person operates the train and he/she only needs to open and close doors and push a button which starts the train from each station. The acceleration and deceleration is automatically controlled and is much smoother than traditional trains.

The stations are unattended although monitored by television from a central location. Fares are collected automatically thereby eliminating the need for cashiers and the handling of money which often encourages violence. The train is quiet, air-conditioned, and on schedule. The complete trip takes 22 minutes including all stops; the same trip takes an hour by car.

The biggest advantage of this system is that people are using it. Surveys have indicated that 40 percent of the 42,000 daily riders had formerly used their cars.

A different system, called the Auto-Train, allows the traveler to drive his/her automobile onto a railroad car. The traveler can then leave the driving to the railroad and have the convenience of the car getting to the station and after the trip. This is a step toward integrating transportation systems and eliminating the necessity of changing modes of travel on a trip. As Hal Ehllmen states, "Today a person taking a trip may have to contend with auto traffic, a bus system, a subway system, a train system, an airline, and perhaps even a ship or ferry."

Bus Travel

The role of buses should not be underemphasized because, at least at the present time, they are the only means of mass transportation that comes close to door-to-door service.

To increase the efficiency of buses, a number of ideas have been put into practice. In some cities buses have, during rush hours, the exclusive right to use certain lanes. Private autos or trucks are not allowed to travel in these reserved traffic lanes and are subject to fines if caught doing so. In Paris the buses operate against the flow of traffic which, as one might imagine, is very effective in keeping motorists out of the bus lanes.

Based upon the theory that it makes more sense to give priority to one bus containing fifty people than twenty cars containing twenty-five or thirty, bus-controlled traffic lights have been installed in some cities. As the bus approaches a traffic light a radio signal device automatically turns the light in the bus's favor. To make sure that two buses traveling in different directions at the same intersection do not collide, the traffic light will only accept a signal from one direction at a time.

Electric Automobiles

While these innovations in bus travel are to be applauded, it must be admitted that most people still prefer to drive their own cars. A determined effort has been made to reduce the amount of pollution each car emits by incorporating emission control devices in automobiles. But the sheer number of cars and trucks is increasing so rapidly that any progress is rapidly undermined. For example, Houston, Texas has an increase of over 400 cars and trucks on its roads every day.

Many people believe that a more direct approach is needed to reduce air pollution caused by the automobile. The electric car is one possibility. It is not a new idea, as it was thought of before the internal combustion engine was created, but the developments in the gas powered car were so rapid that eventually interest in electric cares fell off. It is still true today that the gas powered car can go faster and can travel longer between services. Batteries must, of course, be recharged; and, while a person can travel up to 250 miles on a tank of gas, the electric car must be recharged about every 50 miles. One solution would be a system capable of recharging itself whenever driven into a garage or driveway. An experimental vehicle has already been built which, by using radio signals, can automatically find the nearest electrical outlet and plug itself in.

Assuming that private vehicles are going to be with us for some time in the future, what further developments can we expect? One possibility is to automate the highway. This has usually been thought of as a way of making transportation more convenient for the driver, but it may also be necessary as a means to increase the capacity of the roadways as more and more cars are added every day. If a guideway system were used and designed together with tracks and electric cars, they could go faster with less space between them.

Bay Area Rapid Transit

One of the most well known systems of mass transportation is the Bay Area Rapid Transit (BART) system in San Francisco. With automatic controls each train leaves every 90 seconds at various stations along the 75-mile system. They travel at a maximum speed of 80-mph but are capable of higher speeds. A series of trains traveling at that speed could not safely be coordinated by a human. Automatic controls dispatch the trains, keep them on schedule, open and close the doors, start and stop the trains, and maintain the proper interval between them. As with any new system, there were numerous problems such as cost overruns, labor disputes, and public acceptance but they are being resolved.

Monorails

In a heavily built-up area as most central business districts are, the monorail offers a practical solution to downtown transportation problems. Using support columns the cars can travel above the street or sidewalk and not interfere with automobile or pedestrian traffic. A loop around the heart of the city may be the most logical system because the cars could all move in one direction and take up less room than the normal two-way arrangement. An added advantage is that adverse weather conditions such as snow and sleet do not affect the monorail as it does both air and surface travel.

Tubes and Tunnels

Anyone who does much traveling soon understands the limits of above-ground transportation systems. Snow, fog, rainstorms, hail, sleet, and even tornados and hurricanes all cause periodic problems in all parts of the world. Adverse weather conditions are not only inconvenient but dangerous. The only way to prevent this is to put transportation underground or in some kind of enclosed guideway.

In addition to the problems imposed by weather, there is another reason to consider underground or covered systems. As the speeds of above-ground transportation continues to increase, the danger of collision also becomes greater. And as more and more of the landscape becomes developed, exclusive rights-of-way will become necessary for any mode of above-ground transportation.

One solution to these problems would be to put the system underground. This, however, is not without its problems. Regardless of the shape of the vehicle, if it is in a tube, it will always act like a piston and eventually build up pressure which would keep the vehicle from moving at all. At high speeds the air must be able to move from the front to the rear of the vehicle which leads to problems with air resistance and heat buildup.

One proposal that is being considered is to transfer the air from the front to the back which would produce thrust much the same as a jet engine. The experiment was originally named Project Tubeflight but has been changed to the Air Gulper.

Most serious consideration is being given to the 350- to 400-mph range, but much faster speeds are being considered. A new field of study known as magnetogas-dynamics may provide a method of propulsion based on the interaction of charged gases and magnetic fields to provide thrust. The idea is still in its conceptual stage but advancing rapidly.

To obtain extremely high speeds it would be necessary to create a vacuum in the tube and studies are being conducted which would allow people to travel 2,000 miles per hour through an underground tube.

Personal Rapid Transit

Many transportation planners, seeking a substitute for the automobile, are considering the Personal Rapid Transit (PRT). This system would operate on a track or guideway and the automated vehicles would be no larger than small automobiles. They may also have the capability of operating on both the guideway and street.

The PRT would have many advantages over conventional transit systems. Today's system makes the individual wait for the vehicle: the PRT would wait for the person. Conventional transit makes people stop along the way or transfer to other routes along the way, but the PRT would provide nonstop trips to all riders and would eliminate transfers. Conventional transit is crowded and noisy. With PRT the rider may sit in privacy with a companion and enjoy a smooth, quiet ride. With conventional transit it is difficult, due to economic reasons, to travel in the middle of the night. Not enough people travel at those hours to warrant hiring a driver. The PRT would be available twenty-four hours a day, and during the night when demand is low it could carry cargo. Studies have shown that one PRT could replace about ten automobiles.

The Hydrofoil

The hydrofoil boat, when at rest, looks about like any other craft. The difference is in the wing-like structures that protrude below the bottom and as it picks up speed lifts the craft out of the water in much the same manner as wings provide lift to aircraft. At a certain speed the foils provide enough lifting force to bring the entire craft out of the water and it then proceeds to skim across the surface on the foils. Due to a reduction of resistance, faster speeds are possible and a smoother ride results than with conventional craft.

A similar type of craft, the surface effect ship (SES) operates several feet above the surface but is supported solely on a cushion of air. The Navy foresees an SES as large as an aircraft carrier reaching speeds of 90- and possibly 150-mph.

Cargo Carriers

Thus far we have concentrated on craft that emphasize speed, but size is a trend that must also be considered. Freighters are now carrying 3,500 automobiles but the real giant ships carry oil. These supertankers are so large that new port facilities must be built to accommodate them. Some, in spite of their tremendous size, need only nine people to operate them due to advanced automation.

Commercial Submarines

Based on the development of nuclear-powered ships, submarines, and also sophisticated undersea explorations, the use of submarines for commercial shipping and travel may exist in the future. There has already been a proposal to build a 300,000-ton submarine oil tanker.

In order to justify such tremendous ships there must be some advantages to them. One option is reduction of distance. The present route from Tokyo to London is 12,800 miles, but by traveling under the Artic the voyage is reduced to only 7,500 miles. There is also the advantage of not having to cope with severe weather conditions.

By using different shapes, underwater craft have already reached the speed of 115 miles per hour, and a much higher speed is considered possible. These may come about with the aid of lighter and higher strength materials. New developments in power generation, even beyond that of the current nuclear fission reactors, may supply the necessary power.

V-Ports

The greatest percentage of air travelers make relatively short trips of 500 miles or less. Regardless of the duration of the trip, the same amount of work must be done at both ends of the trip. In addition to the handling of luggage, as much airport space is required by these short trips as longer ones.

These short trips, many of which are by commuters traveling to and from the job, could be handled by other forms of transportation which would be more efficient than using large planes and conventional airports. Copter-planes, capable of vertical takeoff and landing (VTOL), are being proposed which will form a series of air-transport networks within densely populated areas. These VTOL's, with propellers on the ends of their wings, will, when tilted, be able to take off vertically and when desired cruise at normal speeds. If powered by a gas turbine engine, quiet and virtually pollution-free travel will be achieved.

A proposed V-port along the East River in Manhattan, New York, will be eight stories high, cover two large city blocks, and cover a small portion of the river. A 2,000 car parking facility, baggage and handling area, taxi and bus ramps, and connections with hydrofoils will be provided. The VTOL's will land on pods on the roof.

Air Travel

Some years ago the supersonic transport (SST) plane was introduced with the hope of providing passengers with a faster means of travel. But for a number of reasons, mainly environmental, involving noise and air pollution, the SST came under considerable criticism and was eventually, at least in the United States, shelved. Research on the SST continues though; and, if certain problems can be overcome, we are likely to see a revival of it.

A further extension of the SST is the hypersonic transport (HST). It is now in the range of 4,000-5,000 miles per hour. While this seems unbelievable, plans are now being made for aircraft capable of 11,000 miles per hour. Aeronautical engineers working in materials technology are producing substances capable of withstanding the multi-thousand degree temperatures that such speed would produce. At 11,000 miles per hour, no two cities in the entire world would be more than 45 minutes apart.

Cable Television

Cable television originated in isolated or mountainous areas which could not receive good reception of signals coming through the air. A special antenna was usually installed on the highest point available and from this community antenna wires were installed to individual homes. The cable was then connected to the television.

Eventually cable television moved from the scattered rural areas where it was the only means of reception to suburban and city areas which had previously relied on through-the-air transmitters. These transmitters are not only limited in range but can only carry a small number of signals without interfering with each other. The long-range contribution of cable is not its ability to duplicate existing television programs or even to receive selections from up to 50 or more programs. Its major significance is its potential for two-way communication between the home and a large number of information services.

A new development known as fiber optics offers even greater promise than cable. Optical fibers are thin strands of glass that are capable of carrying a large number of signals in the form of pulses of laser light over great distances with little weakening or distortion. More information can be transmitted at the same instant in time through an optical fiber than can be sent by electric current through a wire. A single fiber strand one-fifth the thickness of a human hair could do the work of 10,000 telephone wires or serve as a television cable to transmit 8,000 different channels at the same time.

These new technologies make it possible to bring a vast array of information into one's home and gives that individual the ability to respond with his/her own thoughts, opinions, requests, etc. This is made possible by combining the conventional telephone or television with the computer.

Interactive Television

In a relatively short period of time computers have become lighter, smaller, require less power, and are less expensive. The applications of interactive television in which the viewer has considerable control seem almost limitless. Some of the services it may perform in the home of the future are as follows:

Education: From a library of computer programs the individual would work at his/her own pace in a chosen subject and accomplish established objectives through as many attempts as needed.

Two advantages of this system are the ability to select from a wide variety of courses and the freedom to learn at the convenience of the individual.

Newspaper: The home computer would have access to a large information base but only that information which the viewer wants will be made available. A person who has little interest in local news but is more interested in international news would be presented with only that which is desired. This electronic newspaper could either be viewed on a screen or be printed out on paper with the use of a facsimile machine. At any point the reader may push a button to get more information about the material seen or previously seen.

Business conducted in the home: Many futurists believe there will be a trend toward telecommuting or doing at home (or near home) what has traditionally been done at the office. This may come about due to a variety of reasons. More and more people are now working at clerical or administrative jobs that involve the accumulation and transfer of information rather than the manufacture and movement of material goods. For this reason there is seldom any need for the person to be physically present at their actual place of employment. Furthermore, with an an anticipated reduction of working hours and an increase in pollution and traffic congestion, the idea of working at home may become increasingly appealing.

A considerable amount of business which has previously required costly and time consuming travel could be eliminated by computer conferences. This is similar to a telephone conference call whereby a group of people may converse simultaneously, but there are several advantages to using a computer. By typing messages on the computer the individual may communicate with any number of people and read on the display screen or printout what the others are saying. These invisible meetings can take place twenty-four hours a day with the computer automatically informing the group when someone joins or leaves the discussion. When a person signs off, the computer notes his/her location in the discussion and later picks up at the point where he/she left off. Everyone may "talk" or "listen" at the same time and printout capability provides a permanent record of the proceedings. When it is necessary to travel, the system could provide information on transportation schedules, prices, and hotel availability.

Many services offered by banks could be performed from home by the use of interactive television. Among these services may be arranging for a loan or transferring funds between accounts.

Weather reporting: A much more precise weather report could be received by computer than is presently available. Specific information for the individual could be requested including forecasts for farmers, fishermen, or a particular ski location or vacation resort.

Access to libraries: The reader (or viewer) would have access to certain libraries or information distribution centers. After proper procedures, the desired information could either be projected on the the computer screen or a facsimile could produce it on paper.

Shopping: This system would eliminate the need for physical transfer of cash or checks in financial transactions. Technology exists for electronic reading of identification numbers on credit cards and verification of stolen cards. In the future it will be possible for the prospective buyer, in the comfort of a living room, to view goods on a screen while listening to a description and pricing of it. This would enable the shopper to make instant comparison of prices and characteristics of the product. This electronic catalog could provide up-to-the-minute information on store sales in specified categories and within a distance specified by the viewer.

Entertainment: The potential to entertain may be one of the most appealing features of this new communication system. Whether by cable or satellite, a central video library may offer a wide variety of plays, movies, or documentaries that the viewer may enjoy on a paid subscription basis. This system may also provide information about entertainment events including dates, descriptions, and reviews. The user may even ask for a display of different restaurants, including their menus. Programs offering choices in the thousands may eventually exist.

Holography

One of the most exciting breakthroughs in communications

is holography. Holographic images are produced by laser light, and the finished product, which is called a hologram, is in full color, full size, and three dimensions. These moving projections are amazingly real. When transmitted by satellite they would permit people who are thousands of miles apart to appear to be in the same room.

Satellite Communications

There were about a million overseas telephone calls in 1950. By 1960 there were nearly four million, and six years later the number was up to ten million. One approach to this growth in telecommunications is to lay more and more cables, but they are expensive, both to build and to maintain. Microwave systems are cheaper, but overocean transmission would require incredibly high towers to be built in the middle of the ocean to carry the signal over the curvature of the Earth.

Now, as an offshoot of space technology, satellites seem to offer a solution to many of the problems of previous systems. A satellite stationed 22,000 miles high would orbit Earth in twenty-four hours. Its speed would be at the same rate as Earth's rotation so, in essence, it would remain above a selected location on Earth. At this altitude it would be capable of "seeing" 40 percent of the entire planet. Like an electronic mirror it would accept the upward-bound signal and radiate it back to the appropriate destination.

Thanks to satellites the world has already shared live coverage of sports, debates, and space exploration. Up to this time these services have been enjoyed primarily by the most developed nations. In the future, the underdeveloped countries will also benefit from satellite communications. With existing technology the demand for telephone service in many of these nations far exceeds the ability to supply homes and businesses with efficient communications. This, at present, greatly limits the potential for these nations to advance.

Another area of major importance lies in the distribution of television in underdeveloped countries. A satellite positioned over India could relay entertainment, storm warning, education, and emergency instruction in times of epidemic or other national catastrophe. The major requirements for such a system are one satellite, one major transmitting station, and a large number of low-cost receiving stations. With such plans being developed it becomes easier to imagine the world becoming a system of truly global communications.

Questions for Discussion

1. How do televisions, computers, and satellites, interact in communications systems?

2. Are there disadvantages to using computer systems in education?

3. Would you rather work at home or in an office?

4. Would you like to shop by electronic catalog?

5. Is spending 14 to 18 percent of the family budget on transportation too much?

6. Do the disadvantages of the automobile outweigh the advantages?

7. How serious is the potential invasion of privacy through telecommunications?

Activities

1. Write a scenario about a time when people could no longer discriminate between information, education, and entertainment.

2. Brainstorm ways to fill a multitude of cable television channels.

3. Write a scenario of the paperless office.

4. Develop a cross-impact matrix for various transportation modes of the future.

Primary Sources

Anderson, Edward J. "PRT: Urban Transportation of the Future?" *The Futurist,* Vol. VII (Feb. 1973).

Bagdikian, Ben H. *The Information Machines: Their Impact on Men and the Media.* New York: Harper and Row, 1971.

Baran, Paul. "30 Services that Two-Way Television Can Provide," *The Futurist,* Vol. VII (Oct. 1973).

Clarke, Arthur C. *Profiles of the Future: An Inquiry into the Limits of the Possible.* New York: Harper and Row, 1977.

Futures Research Division, Security Pacific National Bank. "Trends: The Era of the Communications Link", Feb. 1981.

Hellman, Hal. *Transportation in the World of the Future.* New York: M. Evans, 1974.

Hellman, Hal. *Communication is the World of the Future.* New York: M. Evans, 1969.

Hult, John L. "Cheap Communications: How They May Change the Way Men Live," *The Futurist,* Vol. III (June 1969).

Preview

It should surprise no one that we are facing dramatic developments in our habitats. Rising costs of resources, shifting demographics, changing human values, and a volatile economy are major driving forces shaping the future of how and where we live. We are asking ourselves if the "American dream" of private home ownership will prove unattainable as the housing shortage becomes more acute and threatens even the affluent. Between now and the end of the century, construction is expected to fall behind demand formed by the high birth rates of the last few decades. In most of the developing nations even the cheaper housing will be too expensive for one-third to two-thirds of the people. These are distrubing projections that demand attention.

The growth of cities or what is known as urbanization is one of the most obvious trends of the twentieth century. The large cities of today emerged as a result of industrialization and world trade patterns. In 1820 London had a population of one million and by 1900 there were eleven cities throughout the world with a million or more inhabitants. In 1976 there were 191 such cities and it is estimated that by 1985 the million + city will have jumped to 273, with 147 of them in the less developed countries.

Pronounced growth is also seen when considering the ten-million city. In 1950 there were two of them—New York and London. By 1970 there were four of them, and it is forecasted that by 1985 there will be at least seventeen cities with ten million or more people living in them. Ten of these will be in developing nations. Mexico City, for example, will have a projected population of eighteen million inhabitants.

Where are all these people coming from? The major factor is population growth, but demographics show another pronounced trend. In 1900 about 60 percent of the population of the United States lived on farms or in very small towns in the country. Projections indicated that this will reverse itself and by 2000 more than 70 percent of the American people will live in large urban areas. This rural-to-urban shift will continue to have profound effects upon the individual, society, and the landscape of the entire world.

CHAPTER 8

HOUSING/SETTLEMENTS/
URBANIZATION

Old/New Building Techniques

Underground, or "earth-sheltered" homes are currently being constructed and planned at a rate that will soon cause them to loose their novelty status. There are already more than seventy such homes around Spokane, Washington. Earth is an excellent moderator of temperatures, absorbing warmth on a warm day and cold on a cool one. The effect is a narrowing of the temperature range inside the home. Other advantages are a quieter interior, they can be built into slopes, and landscape disturbance is minimal.

The conclusion of World War II made it necessary to build a large number of homes in a short period of time. Prefabrication, a building method that had been in existence for many years, proved to be the best solution to the housing shortage. There are various degrees of prefabrication, but the most common is the manufacture of precut parts in large numbers that are then delivered to the various sites and erected by the builder.

Many builders are now using "curtain-wall" construction for offices and warehouses in which the walls do not support anything but are hung on a steel frame. Panels are then fitted together on the interior to form different environments. Builders claim advantages in cost because of shorter construction time and, because materials are pre-engineered, the builders claim there is structural improvement.

A further extension of prefabrication is modularization based on the idea of a module which is a mass-produced unit of housing or other construction. In this method, a wall, a whole room, or even several rooms are built in a factory, hauled to the site, and installed. This is exemplified by a site in San Antonio, Texas, where each room of a hotel was cast in concrete at a factory several miles from the building site. The inside of each "box" was completely painted, carpeted, and furnished and then lifted into place by a specially built crane. The 500-room, 21-story hotel was built in 202 days, less than half the time conventional construction would have taken.

A similar method involves the erection of a central core in which modules are hoisted into place and then "plugged" into the central tower. It is estimated that the cost for building apartments would be 18 percent less than with conventional methods if a large enough market develops.

Modular homes, offices, schools, and stores offer a unique opportunity for speed, flexibility, and economy in building. They are inexpensive to build, fast to erect, and are easily altered and rearranged. They are not widely seen though because of high transportation costs, the opposition of building trade unions, and the lack of high volume.

New Building Materials

For a number of reasons, including depletion of materials, rising labor costs, and increased demand for land, the cost of building has risen dramatically over the years. This has stimulated the search and use of new, innovative building materials that reduce the need for the 70,000 nails and 30,000 individual parts of the average home.

Concrete has been improved upon by injecting it with a chemical substance while it is being mixed. This causes tiny air bubbles to form in it. This cellular concrete is lighter, stronger, and offers better insulation than conventional concrete.

The fact that plastics are strong, light, pliable, and capable of transmitting light makes them an appealing material for the design of components and entire structures.

Improvements in the composition of steel has allowed the construction of longer spans than ever before. This allows architects greater freedom in the design of buildings.

Urethane foam which was originally developed as an insulation material is now often sprayed on forms which can be of virtually any shape desired. After an earthquake in Turkey, a reusable inflatable plastic mold was sprayed with urethane to serve as shelter for the homeless victims. If made thick enough and designed properly, the structure can be quite strong and serve as a permanent dwelling.

Human Needs

Before moving from the study of the individual dwelling to that of the city, certain basic human needs should be identified. The following considerations should be met through the organization of the city:

1. *Humankind's Physical Needs.* These include food, shelter, sanitation, transportation, places for work, exercise, and some degree of privacy.

2. *Humankind's Love of Nature.* This includes sunshine, fresh air, trees, parks, etc.

3. *Humankind's Need for Societal Interaction.* City facilities will need to include educational, health, and work institutions. The city will need to accommodate the old, the crippled, and to rehabilitate the displaced worker; to have family care services (such as day care); to control juvenile delinquency and crime; and to maintain adequate health and safety standards (such as the control of pests and pollution). A person needs a home and a job he/she can be proud of.

These general needs should be kept in mind while studying the following problems and proposed alternatives in regard to human habitats.

Central Business District Renovation

Traditionally the core are of the city was most important by housing the major cathedral, palace, or town square. It was here where business transactions took place and where people

113

met for social and cultural interaction. The center of the city was, in short, the heartbeat of the city.

After thousands of years this is no longer the case in most cities of the world. The reasons are many and complex. As autombiles and freeway systems developed, people who could afford to, moved from the city to outlying areas and commuted to work. Eventually manufacturing and retailing began to follow this migration and the central business district (CBD) took on a different character. In the 1950's suburban shopping centers began to develop. Today, most suburban dwellers find it unnecessary to travel to the city. As a result, many city centers have been neglected and thus they are dirty, less vital, and even dangerous.

In an effort to reverse this trend many city planners and business entrepreneurs are showing renewed interest in attracting people and investment back to the central business area. As entire blocks are being renovated, people are beginning to appreciate the rich architectural design of many older buildings and ordinary streets which are being transformed into attractive tree and fountain-filled shoppers' paradises. A growing sense of pride and community is beginning to emerge among the people living in these cities.

It should be noted that, while this effort is to be applauded, there is a negative impact to it as well. Prior to renovation the downtown areas have for many years served as the home of the dispossessed poor people of the urban population. It served as an area where they could live cheaply along with people of similar means. Where are they to go when displaced by shoppers and businesspersons? It is a dilemma not easily solved.

Skyscrapers

While growing outward, cities are also growing upward—that is using land more intensively by building taller buildings. The immensity of these skyscrapters can be illustrated by citing some statistics. At present the Sears Tower in Chicago is the world's tallest building at 1450 feet. The World Trade Center, which is one hundred feet shorter, consists of two 110-story towers in which 35,000 people work. Eight thousand visitors come each day on business using one of the 102 elevators per tower. Twelve restaurants serve 20,000 meals a day, and 1000 people are employed cleaning and maintaining the structure.

While providing efficient use of space, some tenants in the upper floors complain of looking down at the clouds. These same residents must telephone downstairs to find out what the weather is like.

Megastructures

Large buildings or complexes known as megastructures are a relatively recent development due to refinements in central heating and air conditioning, elevators, and steel construction.

As with skyscrapers, megastructures are capable of making intensive use of the land, but they also offer an efficient means of interior climate control. The only way that heat is gained or lost is through the exposed surfaces of the building. If a number of units are grouped together, they present less surface space to the hostile environment than separate units. This will save fuel as it will require less heating and cooling and the larger the building, the greater the savings.

Domes

Even before many of the problems of the city were known, R. Buckminster Fuller was transforming visions into practical structures. Based on engineering principles, his geodesic dome is constructed entirely of interlocking triangles and needs no beams or arches to hold it up. The dome is light and strong because it is a portion of a sphere which encloses the most space for the least surface. This in itself makes the geodesic dome one of the most innovative architectural designs of the century.

Fuller originally designed the geodesic dome for small applications such as emergency shelters and small homes, but he believes that technology has reached a level where domes can now be built on a scale of miles rather than feet. It has been proposed that a two-mile area of Manhattan be enclosed. Tremendous amounts of waste heat and cooling energy are lost due to the prevalent systems of individual heating and air conditioning units in buildings which leave their walls and roofs exposed to the elements. It has been estimated that a dome over mid-Manhattan would reduce its energy losses approximately fifty fold.

This would reduce the need for burning coal and oil, thus reducing air pollution. The dome would also prohibit other pollution from entering as well as the noise of passing jets. Just eliminating the need for snow removal may allow the dome to pay for itself within ten years. Rain gutters around the edge could divert and collect much needed rainwater and store it in reservoirs.

It is believed by some that such an environment would give the inhabitants a closed-in feeling. Actually, the structure would be so far from the eyes that it would hardly be noticed, much the same as a screen door seen from a distance. The sky and the stars would not be blocked out unless desired. Modern materials are capable of darkening the panels in bright sunlight as photochromatic sunglasses change from light to dark.

Megalopolis

Anyone who lives in the city or suburbs and finds it increasingly difficult to find a place to fly a kite or go on a picnic may be able to blame urban sprawl. There are many reasons why urban areas are spreading out over the countryside. Some of the reasons are as follows:

1. Overall increase in population.
2. Shift from the farm to the city.
3. Density of the inner city.
4. Deterioration of housing around the core of the city.
5. Rising incomes permitting residents in the inner city to move to the suburbs.
6. Development of extensive highway systems.
7. Industry moving to the suburbs.
8. Development of multicar family.
9. Traffic congestion in the city.

This increasing urbanization or urban sprawl is leading to the development of the megalopolis. The term is derived from two Greek words. "Megalo" means large or great and "polis" means city or city-state. A number of metropolitan areas may overlap to form a megalopolis. It is expected that someday most Americans will be living in one of three areas known as Chi-Pitts (Chicago-Pittsburgh), Bos-Wash (Boston-Washington, D.C.), or San-San (San Francisco-San Diego).

Floating Cities

There are three factors that may encourage the development of floating cities in the years to come. The first is that land is becoming increasingly scarce and costly. This, plus a love of the sea, has already created houseboats, heliports, and the like. The third and most important factor is that over 80 percent of the large metropolitan areas in the United States are located near bodies of water that are deep enough to accommodate floating communities.

The location of floating structures near already existing cities allows the opportunity for using more modern production technology than traditional "on ground" methods. Expense and delay are reduced by building the various units at a shipyard or dry dock and then towing them to their site using the ocean as a highway. The economy and efficiency of shop fabrication can be applied to construction problems which have previously been solvable only at the building site.

Perhaps the key feature of any floating community will be the flexibility allowed by the development of separate modules. Two or three neighborhoods could be installed to eventually form clusters. At any time, units could be added or subtracted as the needs of the city change without causing disruption of the entire structure. This incremental approach eliminates the need to make great expenditures that may not be viable when completed.

The technology necessary to build floating cities already exists and various proposals have already been completed. One plan shows a community protected by a 180-foot high outer protective wall which has been designed to carry even the strongest winds up and over the city leaving the inner area calm. The terraced housing is sheltered from the wind but open to the sun. The entire structure is protected from the ravages of the sea by a breakwater formed by large, anchored bags partially filled with water. This produces a "moat" of calm water around the city.

Many of the inhabitants of a sea city may be engaged in fish farming in which fish could be grown and harvested under controlled, scientific conditions.

Underwater Cities

While floating cities would provide opportunities to study oceanography, it would be limited to shallow water or the top layers of the ocean. If, on the other hand, we are to examine the many mysteries of the ocean, we must go deeper, that is, actually submerge the dwellings.

At present, there are basically two ways to explore the depths. A diver may use scuba gear or work from a submersible, enclosed vehicle such as a bathyscaphe.

There are experiments being conducted which suggest the possibility of obtaining oxygen directly from the water as fish do. If humans achieve the ability to breath underwater, the problem of pressure differences may be overcome because water filled lungs would equalize the pressure inside and out.

Instant Community

According to futurist philosopher F.M. Esfandiary, the cities of the future must be based upon the tremendous mobility of both people and social systems and utilize only the most modern concepts of construction. This means doing away with stones, bricks, steel, or concrete. No material should be used that will last long enough to deteriorate into slums.

He proposes the concept of "instant communities." These would be light, sturdy, and colorful habitations made of aluminum, fiberglass, plexiglass, plastic, and other new building materials. They would be flexible, diverse, and mobile to be able to adapt to a changing society. The design must be oriented to include the most beautiful aspects of nature along with the technology and life styles of the Space Age.

New Towns

With large cities getting bigger and more unmanageable, the problem of how to control growth has become a major concern. One idea is to limit the growth by housing the overspill in separate, small cities rather than allowing the main city to continue growing. The outlying cities are appropriately called new towns and their population and area are preplanned. They are relatively self-contained by being large enough to support diversity, job opportunities, and public facilities. During the planning process the land is divided among that which is to be used for industrial, commerical, and residential purposes. Population density and its relation to open space are also consdiered at this stage. In spite of all the planning though, it must be realized that new towns are not just built but are the result of a process of staged development over a period of time.

New towns have often been very successful at drawing both residents and industry; but the basic objective, remember, was to draw people out of the big cities to reduce overcrowding. The problem is that new towns have been attracting people from all over the surrounding area compounding the problem of density and at the same time reducing available open space.

New Types of Architecture

Aerotectures — Fuller suggests that someday cities may float above the surface of the Earth. In the case of a huge sphere, the sun may heat the enclosed air providing buoyancy. Structures could also be held aloft by currently undeveloped antigravity devices.

Biotectures — If biologists should come to understand how certain organisms can regenerate limbs or organs, architects may take this knowledge and apply it to building methods. It may be possible, for example, to grow a giant rib cage that could serve as the structure for a stadium by using a programmed chemical package derived from biological knowledge.

Agritecture—Green plants may provide living enclosures if shaped by nets, careful pruning, the use of nutrients, and other methods. With greater understanding of growth, certain varieties of plants may even develop naturally into functional dwellings.

Other forms of architecture that today are impractical but could become feasible when unforeseen technologies are discovered and developed include chemitecture formed by using liquid materials which could grow like crystals into structures. With the use of lasers, videotecture may create structures that can be seen but are not made of solid material. People could walk through the "walls" of these structures. Stretching videostructure to its limit, it has been imagined that people may be able to visualize various forms and record—in a yet unknown way—brain wave patterns that the thoughts produced. When converted to sound waves and projected through directional antennas, the imaginary structures would take shape. To produce the same result, sound architecture would create a vibration matrix from which the final form would be solidified. Cybertecture would employ the use of computers to design almost any type of structure in response to human moods by varying the color, light, sound, shape, and size of structures. Finally, cryotecture uses water and other liquids which are thermoplastic; that is, they can change from a solid state to a liquid when heated.

The Need for Planning

The physical arrangements of our cities represent the values of our lives as individuals and as a society. The rapid technological development which has taken place over the last few years has not been matched by thorough planning in our urban areas. By reacting instead of acting upon the future, we have rendered parts of our cities unlivable and unmanageable. Many people have sought refuge in the suburbs only to find that commercialism has spread to the edges of all cities. Planning has often been put aside and left to real estate development, which like any other business, is done for profit. But what is profitable for the entrepreneur may not be advantageous to the whole city. If present development continues, the successful and peaceful future of our urban communities may be very much in doubt.

It is believed by many that nothing less than a complete overhaul of our urban organization is needed. We have the ability to build new communities and they must serve to bridge the gap between rich and poor, white and black, and education and ignorance. Planning of the highest order and on the broadest basis is desperately necessary if our cities are to represent the values of a civilized society.

Questions for Discussion

1. Are cities still the result of industrialization and world trade patterns? Will they change as we move toward post-industrialization?

2. Why is it significant that a large percentage of the fastest growing cities in the world are in the developing nations?

3. How will the rural-to-urban shift affect society?

4. What might Ralph Waldo Emerson have meant when he said that cities make people artificial?

5. What do you consider to be the most basic human needs for a community to meet?

6. What is meant when it is stated that new towns are not just built but are the result of a process of staged development?

7. Should we design our cities to grow vertically, horizontally, both or neither?

8. Would you like to live in a domed city? An "earth-sheltered" home? An underwater city?

9. Are we moving toward the era of instant communities?

10. Is a complete overhaul of our urban organization needed?

Activities

1. Consult a local building contractor and find out how new building materials are being used.

Primary Sources

Esfandiary, F.M. *Up-Wingers: A Futurist Manifesto.* New York: The John Day Co., 1973.

Hellman, Hal. *The City in the World of the Future.* New York: M. Evans, 1970.

Jencks, Charles. *Architecture 2000: Predictions and Methods.*

New York: Praeger Publishers, 1971.

Mason, Roy. "Architecture Beyond 2000," *The Futurist,* Vol. IX (Oct. 1975).

Preview

The universal question of what it means to be human has always occupied our minds. We each have our own concepts of humanness and a consensus has always eluded us. Now, due to new knowledge that is being gained in biomedicine and biopsychology, whole new dimensions have been added to the question. It is a paradox that, while we are unraveling the mysteries of life, we are at the same time being made aware of new questions which are pushing us even further from agreeing on what it is to be human This paradox, which offers both promise and peril, has caused biologist Robert Sinsheimer of California Institute of Technology to proclaim that "our thrusts of inquiry should not too far exceed our perception of their consequences."

In view of the current and potential developments in the medical fields, life extension promises to become a reality. It has been forecast by Alex Comfort, a British gerontologist, that "by 1990 we will know of an experimentally tested way of slowing down age changes in man that offers an increase of twenty percent in life-span." If Comfort's forecast proves true, for Americans, that would raise life expectancies up to about 82 for men and 91 for women.

This chapter illustrates that physical and mental illness, aging, reproduction, behavior, and intelligence are no longer to be considered outside the realm of direct human intervention and control. What does this mean? Brain researcher Jose Delgado suggests that the main question is no longer "What is Man?" but what kind of man are we going to construct?" The questions are many, the implications are awesome, and the challenge is now.

CHAPTER 9

BIOLOGICAL DEVELOPMENTS
& BEHAVIORAL RESEARCH

Reproduction

As humankind began to face overcrowding, food shortages, and social considerations, the task of artificially rectifying the situation was undertaken. Deliberate contraception set us apart from the other inhabitants of the world, but sophisticated methods have only recently appeared. Today the birth control pill is the most widely used contraceptive in the developed nations, and research is now being conducted aimed at developing a "morning after" pill which would eliminate daily intake. A further advancement may be a yearly injection, and it is foreseen that in a short time a male birth control pill will be available.

While many people practice birth control and the methods have become increasingly advanced, there are many who are denied the ability to have children. Fortunately we are now beginning to solve many infertility problems, in part by taking advantage of the knowledge acquired through animal husbandry.

Some years ago the public was informed of some startling research which was being conducted, and in a short time the term "test-tube babies" came into being. Scientists use a less haunting terms—*"in vitro* fertilization" followed by "embryo transplant." The process involves taking a human egg and fertilizing it by a sperm *in vitro,* which means "in glass." This is done in a laboratory, and after the embryo has grown for a few days, it is then implanted in the womb of a female where it continues to develop naturally.

The question arises: why do it? The main reason is to allow an infertile woman to bear a child, but it may also overcome the problem of the male who may have a low sperm count. This being the case, it is difficult to conceive, but under laboratory conditions the egg can be bombarded with thousands of sperm, vastly increasing the odds of fertilization.

The flexibility and real potential of test-tube fertilization and embryo transfer to the womb depends a great deal upon how long eggs and sperm can be kept in storage without deterioration. Cattle ranchers, in the hope of being able to increase their number of livestock, have, since the early 1960's, used frozen sperm from bulls to artificially inseminate cows. Today it is common for a rancher to select and order from a sperm bank. As an offshoot of this technology, human sperm banks emerged in the early 1970's primarily for the purpose of solving specific fertility problems or because of known genetic defects which may be passed on by the male.

If the infertility is due to the woman's reproductive system, it may be possible to implant a frozen egg from a donor. At present, this is much more difficult to achieve than the freezing of sperm. By 1977 at least 1400 babies had been conceived with sperm that had been previously frozen.

If the human embryo can be frozen for storage, which scientists have had little success at, many have envisioned that in a few years a woman might be able to buy a frozen embryo, have it implanted, carry it for nine months, and then give birth to it. Since the embryo had been studied in the laboratory, she could be assured that it would be free of genetic defects. She could also know in advance the baby's physical features and possibly its intelligence quotient (I.Q.).

At some time in the future it may be possible for a woman to have a baby without going through pregnancy. When adoption is either not possible or desirable, a woman may have the embryo transferred to another woman's womb. The

125

surrogate mother would then carry the baby until birth. While this has been successfully achieved in animals, it still presents a formidable challenge in humans. While uncomfortable to contemplate, it has been suggested that nonhuman wombs be used as gestators. According to some embryologists, cows would be the most suitable animals as they have a nine-month gestation period, they don't smoke or eat or drink foolishly, are not overactive, and could be eaten afterwards. And in addition, they do not charge for their services.

Surrogate mothers, whether human or nonhuman, may come to be outdated when artificial wombs are perfected. Today, hundreds of scientists are attempting to achieve this, but it is difficult to replicate the natural womb and placenta in all their complexity.

There may be any number of medical reasons why a woman should not or cannot carry a baby to birth. To do so may be risky not only for her but for the baby. There may also be nonmedical motives. Perhaps it would detrimentally affect her career to go through pregnancy. A public personality such as an actress or singer may not wish to lose her figure and possibly her public image. It may also be a case of just not wanting to go through the ordeal of childbirth.

Of all the recent developments in the field of embryology, the predetermination of a baby's sex may be the most talked about. To date, scientists have considered at least a dozen ways of doing this. Some are more accurate and less risky than others, but none of them have been perfected or widely used.

Transplantation of Limbs and Organs

Every year approximately 867,000 people die as the result of the breakdown of a single organ and the complications that result. Many more continue to live but only with tremendous suffering, grief, and financial strain. One way to help overcome this is by the transplantation of limbs and organs.

After years of experimentation by a number of scientists

and doctors, a successful kidney transplant was performed in 1954. The donor and recipient were twin brothers as, at the time, no transplants between unrelated people had been successful. Today there are thousands of people leading normal lives after kidney transplants, and the overall success rate continues to improve.

Progress is being made in the transplantation of other organs including lungs, livers, corneas, intestines, limbs, and the heart. The world was shocked when, on December 2, 1967, the heart of a critically injured woman was used to replace that of a terminally ill heart patient. The man lived for nearly a month, and the autopsy revealed that he died of pneumonia caused by drugs used to prevent natural rejection of the foreign heart tissue. Getting the body to accept the new organ continues to hinder the success of transplant operations, but researchers are making headway in immunosuppression—the medical term for preventing the rejection response.

Even if immunosuppression can be achieved, it is difficult, except in unique instances, to provide organs at the time they are needed and in a healthy condition. Living donors are the most desirable as the organs are usually healthy, but few people are willing to donate unless to a relative. The dead body or cadaver, as it is medically called, is less satisfactory because death normally harms most organs and any delay causes rapid deterioration. Animal organs could be used, and they are more available but are not as readily accepted by the human body.

As a result of these problems, artificial materials have been developed and used to replace bones and joints; but, when the passage of blood is involved, the challenge becomes greater. Nevertheless, implantable artificial hearts are being developed with self-contained nuclear drive systems. Artificial kidneys are now in wide use, but they are large and cannot be implanted.

The perfection of artificial organs and the storage of natural ones are still beyond the ability of today's researchers, but there is an alternative. The idea of using "living cadavers" is being proposed as a means of supplying organs and conducting research. These bodies would be legally dead as any electrical brain activity would have ceased, but they would continue to breathe, excrete, and require feeding and nursing. Neomorts, as they would be called, could help save lives and advance medical knowledge by allowing medical students to practice routine examinations, spinal taps, skin grafts, organ removal, and other types of surgery. Diseases could be induced, treatment and drugs tried, and any breakthroughs could be made available to the public years before they could using conventional methods. Body organs, limbs, and blood could be catalogued and computerized according to compatibility in bioemporiums—hospitals or wards for harvesting the dead.

Someday, bioemporiums may be of less utility if biologists continue their successful research in limb and organ regeneration. Some animals that are close to us in evolutionary terms can grow their own spare parts, and scientists have been studying this ability for many years. Techniques using drugs, electrical stimulation, or both have already been used to promote regeneration in animals, and it seems only a matter of time before they are applied to humans.

Cybernation

Cyborg, an abbreviation for "cybernetic organism," is a word that has only recently joined our vocabulary. As defined by Dr. Manfred Clynes, a research scientist is the field of cybernetics, a cyborg is an "exogenously extended organization complex functioning as an integrated homeostatic system unconsciously." To put it in simpler terms, a cyborg is the product of joining a living thing with a nonliving device or devices.

To stretch the definition to its limit, it could be said that a person with a wooden leg is a cyborg. So is a person wearing glasses, writing with a pen, or driving an automobile. These simple examples all represent extensions of the human being but are not so sophisticated as to cause us to question what it means to be human in a time when humans and machines are becoming more closely associated.

Initiated by the U.S. Navy and Air Force, research is being conducted to develop a "man-amplifier" in which a person wears a steel "exoskeleton" powered by hydrolics instead of muscles. The mechanical frame will mimic the user's movements but with added strength. Preliminary designs are aimed at allowing either arm to lift a thousand pounds, but eventually the ability to lift an automobile may be child's play.

Cyborgs are not tools in the sense that, unlike a fork or a wrench, communication between the user and the tool is two-way. A wooden leg is unable to respond to stimuli and is thus unable to function as a natural leg would. For the same reason a mechanical arm or manipulator may crush a golf ball when attempting to pick it up. The ability to provide feedback, which allows strength and dexterity, is a key challenge to prosthetics, the study of artificial devices to replace or supplement parts of the body.

In the case of amputated limbs, progress is being made by implanting electrodes in the remaining muscles to act on the natural electrical signal which is generated in the muscle when the person thinks about a desired movement. These signals are called myoelectric (myo is Greek for muscle) and allow a paralyzed person or amputee mobility and a wider range of activities.

To aid blind people, scientists are now using miniature television cameras whose images are then transmitted to nerves in the stomach through a waistband instrument. These nerves send a picture pattern to the brain, which then activates the visual center and provides sight.

The merging of human and machine can be taken to a further stage based on the current ability to maintain the brain outside of the body. The brain may be placed in an artificial "body" equipped with the necessary devices to maintain the "natural" brain thus bringing into being total, or near total, prosthesis. While this may be decades in the making, it cannot be easily dismissed as fantasy; and, combined with computers, the possibilities seem almost infinite.

Cryonics

Long a favorite theme for science fiction writers, the notion of freezing the human body has recently gained new popularity. The technique of human hibernation emerged about the time of World War II and is termed cryonics, cryobiology, or cryogenics. Much of our knowledge of it comes from studying hypothermia, which is the lowering of body temperature and allows animals to hibernate by slowing down the metabolism which supplies the cells with energy.

Since 1967, about 50 people have been frozen in the United States. Their bodies have been packed in dry ice, their blood has been drained, and they have been injected with glycerol and DMSO (dimethylsulfoxide) to prevent ice crystals from forming and damaging the cells. They are stored at -320 degrees Fahrenheit.

Why have they done this? Most of them were suffering from an incurable disease and hope to be preserved until a cure is found. If the process is ever perfected, one may choose to be frozen simply in order to be able to witness the world in the future.

It must be remembered though that, even if the cause of death can be cured by advances in medical science, the body still has to be thawed out. At present this is not possible, but extensive research is being conducted with some limited success.

Genetics

"Life is beginning to cease to be a mystery," according to Professor J.D. Bernal, "and becoming practically a cryptogram, a puzzle, a code that can be broken, a working model that can sooner or later be made."

Most people consider life in almost mystical terms, so complex and awesome as to be beyond human understanding. The scientist sees living organisms as intricate machines that can be disassembled, rearranged, and even artificially created. With human curiosity as the driving force and increasingly sophisticated technology and accumulated knowledge, we are being thrust into a new biological epoch. The genetic philosopher Theodosius Dobzhansky has written that the emerging genetic technology "would represent an instrument of scarcely imaginable power for guidance of the evolution of the human species."

The modern study of genetics, the branch of biology dealing with heredity and its variations, began in the mid-1880s by Gregor Mendel. An Austrian monk and botanist, Mendel worked out the basic universal laws of genetics by conducting research on pea plants. He deduced that there must be a unit of some type that transmitted ancestrial characteristics over generations. At the time, this was all that was known and later these physical substances were called genes (from the Greek word for "reproduction").

For many years it was thought that genes were composed of protein, but in 1944 it was discovered that they were made up of long chains of atoms called DNA (deoxyribonucleic acid). This discovery caused tremendous excitement among scientists around the world, and knowledge of the secret of its operation was the new goal. The best analogy to DNA is the tape in a tape recorder or computer. They both "tell" the device how to operate or, in the case of living organisms, it tells each individual cell how to function at any one moment.

Finally, in 1953, James D. Watson and Francis H.C. Crick, by combining the research of others, formulated an idea of the structure of DNA. The model showed that genes, which are composed of DNA, operate to produce the characteristics in a cell by producing RNA (ribonucleic acid). RNA acts as a "messenger" instructing the cells what to do by producing different proteins which keep cells alive.

Since its inception, the knowledge gained in genetics has contributed to eugenics, the science dealing with the improvement of hereditary qualities. Eugenic engineering has several aspects, many of which are controversial. The field is divided into negative eugenics, which aims at reducing the number of defective genes in human society by screening of babies or aspiring parents. Positive eugenics, on the other hand, involves efforts to produce improved or novel human forms.

Negative eugenics may take a variety of forms including compulsory counseling, compulsory sterilization, denial of the right to bear children without a license, and screening of newborns to spot genetic defects. Some persons are of the opinion that with the new knowledge in genetics, measures such as these should be initiated in order to reduce the number of genetically unhealthy people. It is believed by a number of well-known biologists that the human gene pool is deteriorating and resulting in more genetically caused ailments. They cite the advancement of medicine as the primary cause because now we are keeping people alive who, in the past, would not have lived and passed on genetic impairments to their children.

Genetic mutations are on the rise due to increasing amounts of radiation in our environment which triggers gene mutations. The radiation comes from the fallout of nuclear test explosions, nuclear energy plants, X-rays, and perhaps television.

A more controversial assertion is that there is a trend toward genetically induced dull-wittedness. Throughout history natural selection has tended to allow the mentally superior a better chance of surviving. Today it is sometimes argued that these brighter people are having fewer children than those with less mental ability who tend to have larger families. In addition to family patterns, our entire life style undermines natural selection as automobiles, heating and air conditioning, and kitchen conveniences make it easier for the physically weak to survive and be genetic carriers.

The concept of positive eugenics was captured by Sir Francis Galton at the turn of the twentieth century when he stated, "It has now become a serious necessity to better the breed of the human race." Positive eugenics, a more radical idea than negative eugenics, may allow us to transform humankind through various approaches.

Techniques such as gene surgery, gene copying, gene insertion, and gene deletion are being refined. Dr. Edward L. Tatum, a Nobel Prize winner, has described genetic engineering as, "the most astounding prospect so far suggested by science." It is being presumed by scientists within the field that we are rapidly approaching a time when the limits to remaking ourselves are only bound by the imagination or dictates of a changing environment. By the manipulation of DNA, for example, it may be possible to grow smaller, to breathe under water through gills, to live in different atmospheres in space, and many other possibilities.

If this sounds like science fiction, consider the remarkable transformation from tadpoles into frogs or from caterpillars into butterflies. These are all carried out naturally through the genetic code. Imagine what may take place when we are able to manipulate the code through direct intervention.

Cloning

Of all the possibilities that genetic engineering may offer, cloning could be the most bizzare with mindstretching implications for the future. The word "clone" comes from the Greek word for "slip" or "twig," implying reproduction from cuttings as is common in gardening.

All the information for an organism is contained within the genetic structure of a single cell. If this cell can be made to divide into more cells, it will completely reproduce the organism from which it was taken. The result is an identical twin with exactly the same features, whether plant, animal, or human. As a result, organ transplants between the original and the clone would not be rejected. It is even possible that organs could be grown outside of the body from a cell of the person needing it. People could then arrange, through cell banks, to have organs of their exact genotype available for transplant.

Frogs have been successfully cloned by taking a cell from the intestine, removing the nucleus, and then removing the nucleus from a female frog egg cell and replacing it with the nucleus from the adult frog cell. The method is not as simple for humans as it is in plants or frogs. For one thing, the frog egg is very large and can be more easily manipulated than the human egg, which is very delicate and susceptible to traumatic injury. Secondly, a human egg must be incubated inside a womb, and at present the reinsertion of a human egg is very difficult.

Biopsychology

The research that is being carried out by technologists in the fields of behavioral, biological, and computer sciences reflects a dramatic ability to reshape people and their behavior. B.F. Skinner, a noted behaviorist of Harvard University, has proposed "a technology of behavior" because "we need to make vast changes in human behavior." A few years ago, in trying to describe what behavioral engineering is, a group of psychologists explained, "For openers, we can develop a technology for routinely producing superior human beings...

We have the technology for installing any behavior we want." In the opinion of some, including Aldous Huxley, even after considering the magnitude of the many religious, political, and economic revolutions humankind has witnessed, none will compare to the biopsychological revolution toward which we are rapidly moving. It has been suggested that, when it is over, the human race will give no further trouble. Other knowledgeable people in the field are more cautious and consider it an arrogant presumption that scientists think they are wise enough to remake humankind.

Whatever one's opinion on the feasibility or desirability of biopsychological techniques, it is generally agreed that such research shows that humans are very malleable. We are all susceptible to manipulation, modification, and control.

Mood altering drugs have become a way of life for many people. It is a rare person who does not, at least occasionally, use some type of substance to induce a mood change whether it be through stimulants, tranquilizers, depressants, narcotics, or hallucinogens.

For centuries, various substances have been ingested for different purposes, but only now are we confronted with a radically new dimension of drug use. They can now be used to program people, which means getting others to act as consistently as you want them to act. Some scientists are so confident of the manipulative powers of the new drugs that they call for research on how to chemically control the behavior of political leaders. Kenneth B. Clark, in a speech to the American Psychological Association, stated that powerful political figures might wish to improve their control over the behavior of subordinates or the masses.

Just as drugs or chemicals can alter the mind and behavior, so can electricity. This is because the brain is composed of billions of interconnected neurons which are triggered by electrical or chemical influences. Electrical stimulation of the brain (ESB) involves surgically implanting thin wire electrodes into the brain. They can then be used to stimulate neurons in specific areas of the brain by switching an electric current on or off.

In humans, ESB can stimulate the closing of the hand into a fist, even if the subject does not cooperate. Beyond such motor effects, ESB can also be used to stimulate pleasure, pain, aggressiveness, or pacifism. Jose M.R. Delgado, a pioneer in brain probing, once rigged a bull for radio-controlled ESB. He faced the animal, and when the bull went into its charge he pushed a button. The bull immediately came to a halt and walked away. Based on such experiments, most of which are not as dramatic, research is being conducted on humans. The demand is there as many institutions are eagerly looking for ways to change the behavior of people they must deal with.

Through ESB researchers have demonstrated that memories can be revived almost as if a movie were being played back in the mind. It seems that the brain never loses any of the facts or impressions that enter it, but we are just unable to recall them when desired. When it is discovered how the brain stores all its impressions, we may gain conscious or artificial control of our memory.

What can we conclude about this new technology that allows us to modify mood and behavior by electrical or chemical means? Much of the research has led to the cause and possible cure of ailments such as insomnia, overeating, epilepsy, pain, Parkinson's disease, and forms of mental disorder. Experimentation that advances knowledge and that is used for such application can be applauded, but are there other implications and applications that should be considered? It seems a sad truth that knowledge always comes as a two-edged sword. The advances in biomedicine that have taken place and the capabilities that are looming in the future promise to transcend human beings from creature to creator; but, if this is desired, there are many perils that accompany the promise. "As we stand at the threshold of the chemopsychiatric era and look towards the future," Dr. Robert deRopp has written, "some may feel disposed to cheer and some to shudder."

The Biological Revolution has the potential to influence our lives, our society, and future generations in ways that may be very adverse. One of the most haunting is its ability to control another person's brain against his or her will. In a world where most of us are followers and only a few are leaders, it may be possible for a minority to exert a large degree of control over the majority through biopsychological techniques.

Scientists have amassed a large amount of knowledge and understanding about the effect of mood-altering drugs on the individual, but what is not known is the overall effect on society. Will the continued use of tranquilizers have the long-term effect of lowering ambition and creativity of society? Is it socially healthy for millions of people to expect to achieve continual bliss by taking psychotropic drugs?

In the last twenty-five years, scientists have synthesized a number of mind-altering drugs, the most notable being LSD. In 1975 a national commission found that the Central Intelligence Agency (CIA) was administering such drugs without the subject's awareness. One case allegedly led to suicide. Is it ridiculous to assume that chemicals would never be added to our drinking water without our knowing it? Could concentrated substances be poured into reservoirs by authorities in times of social unrest? Chemicals that produce suggestibility in the individual could be added during propaganda campaigns. Conversly, the ruling powers may deem it necessary to arouse aggressiveness on a mass scale in times of war or a perceived threat.

In addition to drugs, which can be applied on a massive scale, psychosurgery is sometimes used on people in prisons, mental institutions, and homes for the aged. The rationale for surgically operating on the brain used to be in order to relieve the patient of extreme aggressiveness. It is now often being used to make patients or inmates more docile and controllable whether or not they are dangerous to others or to themselves. Robert Neville, while heading a task force formed by the Institute of Society, Ethics and the Life Sciences, concluded that psychosurgery has a dangerous attraction for institutions as "the cheapest and easiest treatment to adopt for controlling patients." This raises the possibility of using psychosurgery to subdue aggressive political dissidents.

In a totalitarian system, selected people may be forced to have two electrodes planted into their brains. One would stimulate a pleasure center; the other, a pain center. Using these as positive and negative reinforcement, the controller would be able to control certain behaviors.

Most people would like to be more intelligent and the drug companies know it. Psychoneurobiochemists are discovering more about what intelligence is, and these breakthroughs may lead to the production of an I.Q. pill. Will there be a great rush to obtain these get-smart pills? Of great importance is how they will be distributed. Most probably they will, at least initially, be quite expensive. What are the implications of this?

Questions such as these have led an appreciable number of scientists to believe that their discoveries are not automatic boons to humankind. This recent change of attitude is evident by the greater amount of debate among themselves as to the wisdom of what they are doing. Ethicists, theologians, public servants, and philosophers are beginning to share views with those in the scientific and medical fields for the issues are far too important to be left solely in the hands of the researchers.

In 1969, a team of brilliant young Harvard researchers, headed by Jonathan Beckwith, called a news conference. They had just isolated the first gene in history. In a somber tone one of them stated, "We do not have the right to pat ourselves on the back" because in the long term the discovery might "loose more evil than good" upon humankind. This speculation demands that we begin to arrive at value judgments on whether proposed biomedical technologies will contribute to or undermine sound social policy.

Questions for Discussion

1. Should a method for predetermining a baby's sex be perfected?

2. Should bioemporiums be established?

3. Should cryonics be perfected?

4. What are some examples of negative eugencis? To what extent should these be practiced?

5. Do you agree with Sir Francis Galton's statement that, "It has now become a serious necessity to better the breed of the human race?"

6. Dr. Edward L. Tatum has suggested that genetic engineering is, "the most astounding prospect so far suggested by science." Do your agree?

7. Should cloning be perfected?

8. Do we need, as B.F. Skinner believes, to make vast changes in human behavior?

9. How malleable are we?

10. Is knowledge always a two-edged sword?

11. Dr. Robert deRopp has written, "As we stand at the threshold of the chemopsychiatric era and look toward the future, some may feel disposed to cheer and some to shudder." How do you respond?

12. Should an I.Q. pill be developed?

13. Would you want to specify everything about the genetic makeup of your child prior to birth?

14. Would you deliberately choose to have a child with a very high I.Q.?

15. Do you want to know what your chances would be of procreating a defective child?

16. If you knew your chances of having a seriously defective child were one out of four, would you choose to have a baby?

17. Should we as a society deliberately try to improve the human species.

Activities

1. Complete a futures wheel centered on the implications of significant life extension.

2. Brainstorm ways in which the human body could be improved.

3. Write a scenario focusing on environmentally induced genetic mutations.

4. Develop a cross-impact analysis on a form of negative eugenics such as compulsory counseling.

5. Construct a decision tree with the goal of less genetically induced impairments in society.

6. Conduct a Delphi poll dealing with how and to what extent cloning should be exercised in the future.

7. Write a scenario about a society in which electrodes have been planted in the brain.

8. You are a member of a medical task force and must decide how I.Q. pills will be distributed. They are now perfected and are inexpensive, but production is very limited and will continue to be for some time. Who will get them and on what basis?

9. You are a brilliant young geneticist engaged in various research activities. Write a speech appealing for the right to

conduct unrestrained research.

10. Complete a cross-impact analysis on memory control.

Primary Sources

Augenstein, L.G. *Come Let Us Play God*. New York: Harper and Row, 1969.

Halacy, Daniel S. *Genetic Revolution: Shaping Life for Tomorrow*. New York: Harper and Row, 1974.

Hellman, Hal. *Biology in the World of the Future*. New York: M. Evans, 1971.

Kurtzman, Joel, and Gordon, Phillip. *No More Dying: The Conquest of Aging and the Extension of Human Life*. Los Angeles: J.P. Tarcher, Inc., 1976.

Rosenfeld, Albert. *The Second Genesis: The Coming Control of Life*. Englewood Cliffs, N.J.: Prentice-Hall, 1969.

Rosenfeld, Albert. *Prolongevity*. New York: Alfred A. Knopf, 1976.

Taylor, Gordon. *The Biological Time Bomb*. New York: World Publishing Co., 1968.

Young, David P. *A New World in the Morning: The Biopsychological Revolution*. Philadelphia: Westminster, 1972.

Preview

Futurists have long been fond of stating that history need not repeat itself. There have been enough wars, economic calamities, and general social malaise throughout history that to think of this as being a continual process would seem too pessimistic. Until quite recently, to be pessimistic was close to being deemed a "traitor" to futuristics. Futurists, it seemed, were supposed to be optimistic defenders of humankind's ability to create a more desirable future. If these two criteria—being optimistic and believing that we can create our own future—define a futurist, there are now fewer of them in existence than during any previous time. Pessimism seems particularly warranted in regard to our economic future, although history suggests that waves of pessimism can arise less as a correct reading of the long-term future than as a response to contempory conditions.

CHAPTER 10

ECONOMICS

The Kondratieff Wave

The 50th anniversary of the Great Depression was in 1979 and was marked by a resurgence of interest in the theory of a Russian economist. Nickola Kondratieff, whose major work appeared in the mid-1920's, describes a business cycle that extends over a 45-60 year period. The Knodratieff Wave is marked by three distinct phases. The first phase is a long (approximately 30 years) period of economic growth. This gives way to a time when prices & economic activity tend to flatten out. The third stage is one of dwindling economic activity and falling prices. Short bouts of recession or expansion may occur within each of the periods but they will be short-term occurrences, all failing to alter the major trend.

Jay W. Forrester, an economist from the Massachusetts Institute of Technology, recently initiated a computer-based study to examine the relevance of the Kondratieff Wave to the current economic climate. The National Systems Dynamic Model represents a multitude of economic segments and interactions acting as a role-playing replica of the real economy. The output of the Model correlates so closely with the long-wave behavior of the Knodratieff Wave, and what is now occurring in the United States and other Western industrialized nations, that a great many economists and social scientists are beginning to express concern. By most indications we are at the peak of the wave, characterized by a decline in capital investment, rising unemployment, a leveling of labor productivity, falling rate on investment, and other key factors. Similar conditions occurred in the 1920's when the wave previously reached its peak. At that time, prices were

143

rising dramatically, debts were high, and the financial system was overextended. Basically the same conditions existed during the depressions of the 1830's and the 1890's. Thus, both the National Model and historical analysis seem to promise another period of depression in the 1980's.

Those who remember the Great Depression know how much an economic crash affects the social and political environment. Their jobs, wages, assets, family life, and overall expectations changed so drastically that many still cannot feel totally secure. The younger members of our society, on the other hand, have experienced general prosperity and affluence making it difficult to envision and prepare for a more difficult future.

Economic indicators aside, there are a number of social signals that may be evidence of hard times ahead. A new social mood is emerging, one that is reminiscent of the early 1900's. People are becoming more cautious, more "traditional," more religious, less hedonistic, and there is more talk of "the good old days." Our changing social norms seem to be telling us something.

To believe in the Kondratieff Wave is to admit, at least to some degree, that history does repeat itself. Can we still be optimistic? We can if we extend our time frame to the recovery years, recognizing that capitalism and technological innovation both seem to require periodical recuperation from exhilarating growth. It is possible that our technology has reached maturity and, at least in the near-term, we cannot anticipate any radical innovations comparable to aircraft, antibiotics, or computers. We may have to wait until the next technological wave built upon a new social-economic thrust. According to Forrester, we should now be looking ahead to this next period that could emerge in approximately 20 years.

Post-Industrial Society

Modern industrialization is composed of three basic

sectors: farming and mining, manufacturing, and service. According to some experts, we are now in the midst of a historic transition comparable in magnitude to the agricultural and industrial revolutions. Today's economic structure is the reflection of a gradual but significant shift toward the service sector composed of educators, doctors, bankers, computer programmers, and other livelihoods not involved in the direct production of material goods. In the technological sector, new science-based industries predominate, adding to the service-oriented society involving almost two-thirds of the work force. The increased levels of affluence, education, and technology cannot be denied, but it is questionable as to whether, as the adherents to post-industrialism expect, that this will necessarily lead to radical new departures from the past. Will a continuation of the post-industrial trend lead to our being able to produce all our material needs and wants with less than a quarter of our work force, as some are forecasting?

The vision of greater affluence, shorter work weeks, less industry accompanied by more services, and an increase in the number of white collar jobs may be undermined by the call for reindustrialization. In an environment besieged by rising energy costs, declining productivity, and aged industrial machinery we may be forced, at least during the 1980's, to postpone post-industrialism. Instead of transcending farming, mining, and manufacturing we may end up restoring them. Could our inability to achieve a truly post-industrial society be the precursor to an economic depression for the next 10-20 years? If so, will we at the conclusion of it find ourselves in a better position to capitalize on what may then be the next phase of technological innovation that is, at present, beyond our ability to achieve? So many areas in the technological sphere, from biotechnology to electronics to artificial intelligence appear to be awaiting a new social-political-economic environment that will propel us into a new era. It is not likely to occur during an economic depression. Perhaps history must repeat itself once more.

Questions for Discussion

1. To what extent is history going to repeat itself?
2. Would the next economic depression be worse than the ιast one?
3. How can the individual prepare for a depression?
4. Can post-industrialization emerge during difficult economic times?
5. Has our technological superstructure reached maturity?

Activities

1. Write a scenario describing how we escaped a depression.
2. Prepare a personal contingency plan in case of economic breakdown.

Primary Sources

Cornish, Edward. "The Great Depression of the 1980's: Could it Really Happen?" *The Futurist* Vol. XIII (October 1979).

Forrester, Jay W. "A Great Depression Ahead? Changing Economic Patterns." *The Futurist* Vol. XIII (December 1978).

Hamil, Ralph. "Is the Wave of the Future a Kondratieff?" *The Futurist* Vol. XIII (October 1979).

Heilbroner, Robert L. *Business Civilization in Decline.* New York: W.W. Norton & Co., 1976.

Preview

It is a sad irony that while all nations and peoples desire security, world security continues to erode and humans seem to exercise their greatest ingenuity in developing new and more dangerous technologies. One nation develops a new weapon because they feel insecure. Another nation develops a new weapon because they feel insecure due to the new weapon. The other nation again feels insecure and develops a new weapon and so on and so on and so on. How secure are we living under the "balance of terror" that has emerged within the last thirty years? Have we resigned ourselves to the possibility of nuclear war in which unimaginable destruction and suffering may result? In a war in which each nation is capable of destroying each other in thirty minutes, is there a difference between defense and offense?

Many people are now beginning to question the sanity of the global arms race and are seeking alternatives which would be less ruinous, less costly, and more equitable as means to resolve international differences. Going beyond the possible resolution of the global arms madness and including an attack on world poverty, repression and injustice, and ecological deterioration is "world order." Traditionally, "international relations" has primarily focused on the patterns of authority and decisions of major governments. "World order" seeks a more comprehensive view by realizing the influence and interaction of not only governments but various international institutions such as corporations, labor unions, religious groups, and political parties. Inherent in the values of a world order is the belief that global reform must be brought from utopian fantasy to practical politics. As Leon Eisenberg said, "The idea of brotherhood is not new, but what is special to our times is that brotherhood has become the precondition for survival."

CHAPTER 11

WORLD ORDER

The Need for World Order

The birth of a new world order is seen by many to be both desirable and necessary for reasons that are less spectacular but just as threatening as nuclear exchange. All of them stem from the realization that no nation can any longer assure the security and well-being of its people.

The first reason is that international order is becoming increasingly difficult to maintain in a world comprised of over 150 sovereign nations, all interacting in a variety of ways over numerous issues. This complexity, involving a multitude of groups and individuals, all with differently perceived priorities, capabilities, and positions, is making it impossible to reach consensus through traditional modes of diplomacy. The need for some form of centralized political management is becoming obvious.

Secondly, there is a growing appreciation for the need of a more cooperative framework in which interdependence can flourish without upsetting the economic, political, and ecological systems of the world. In a world that is getting "smaller," we are now beginning to realize the crucial importance of global cooperation that must include relations between rich and poor, large and small.

Finally, modern technology is superseding national boundaries. The development of weather modification, mining of the ocean floor, large-scale ecological disruption, and satellite surveilance are only some examples of technologies that are not limited to the country of origin. National governments are finding it more difficult to resolve the problems these developments often bring with the only recourse sometimes being armed conflict.

Main Problem Areas

In an effort to bring about a level of order in planetary politics, these main problem areas are being studied:

1. *Poverty:* poor nations as a whole and the poor within affluent nations. World order value: economic well-being.

2. *Repression and injustice:* as applied to individuals within a nation and entire nations. World order value: social and political justice.

3. *Ecological deterioration:* affecting individuals, nations, and the planet. World order value: ecological balance.

4. *The war system:* force being prevalent within the nation and occupying a prime role in international policies, the arms race, the impotence of peacekeeping institutions. World order value: peace.

It is estimated that more than half of the world's population is presently hungry and over two-thirds is undernourished. Starvation, disease, illiteracy, poor sanitation, and generalized deprivation are the lot of most people living in the Third World. Along with this exists the affluence of the developed world where waste is abundant and advertising encourages superfluous consumption. The present organization of the world economic system, with its patterns of trade and investment, sometimes preserves the inequitable distribution of the Gross Global Product.

The main objective of the realization of human rights and political justice is to assure conditions that will allow individual and group dignity within national societies. The prevention of genocide, the drastic modification of racist regimes, the elimination of all forms of torture and cruelty, and progress toward equality of treatment for different races, sexes, ages, religions, tribes, and political groups are all principle dimensions in the effort to create a just world order.

The areas of environmental quality is a multi-faceted and complicated affair embracing both the containment of pollution and the conservation of resource stocks. The problem areas are many, but the following preliminary steps may, upon effective implementation, help insure global environmental quality:

● The initiation of data collection to permit intelligent assessments of ecological problems.

● The establishment of early-warning systems.

● The assessment of the environmental effects of high technology such as the supersonic transport (SST), nuclear testing, and toxic waste disposal.

● The codification and strengthening of international arrangements with respect to ecological issues.

● Long-range forecasting of resource shortages.

Imperative to a better system of world order is the reduction of large-scale collective violence. This involves not only less reliance upon violence and war as a basis for national security and the resolution of conflict but also the development of a credible set of substitute mechanisms. Assuming that in at least the near to intermediate future there will still exist conflict and tension in the world, new settlement techniques must be developed which could take over the role presently filled by the war system. Workable adjudicative and conciliatory mechanisms and means to assure their implementation are necessary. These structural reforms will not be effective unless supported by an upsurge in the ethics of nonviolence and the belief that these means can be used on a larger scale than is the case today. We must strive for a cumulative experience of conflict resolution whereby individuals and groups take pride in eliminating conflict.

The War System

A few statistics will indicate the high priority that military endeavors maintain throughout the world.

● Since World War II, nations have spent more than six trillion dollars for armaments.

● The world's annual military expenditures are now $370 billion.

● At present levels of military spending, the average person can expect over his/her lifetime to give up three to four years' income to the arms race.

● Six trillion dollars is equivalent to an investment of $1500 for every man, woman, and child living today.

● World military expenditures are increasing at an annual rate of about 4.5 percent.

● The world's military spending now amounts to a million dollars a minute.

● In two days the world spends on arms the equivalent of a year's budget for the United Nations and its specialized agencies.

● Approximately 125 thousand American scientists are engaged in research and development of devices and systems with military applications. That is about one in every four.

The United States and the Soviet Union now have the potential for deploying seven thousand times the explosive power that was used by all nations in World War II. The blockbuster bomb used at that time had a power of ten tons of TNT. The nuclear bomb that was dropped on Hiroshima in 1945 was equivalent to thirteen thousand tons of TNT. Today a single nuclear warhead may have an explosive force of up to twenty-five million tons of TNT. These figures reach beyond the ability of human imagination, but it makes the threat no less real.

The increase in the explosive force of weapons indicates the tremendous change which has occurred in military technology since the end of the Second World War. What have some of these changes been and what trends can be identified?

Occupying a major role in the field of military research and development is the trend toward increasing precision in the arming and controlling of weapons. The work being done in this area ranges from improved rifle sights through the use of lasers for air-to-ground missile guidance. Error of less than one hundred meters for intercontinental missiles is now plausible. Video systems placed in the noses of missiles and greater accuracy in satellite photography are improving targeting. Greater precision in guidance is also being achieved through a recently developed system called TERCOM (Terrain Contour Mapping). This system, built into the projectile, scans the ground it is traveling over with a radar beam and, by measuring the distance of the ground as it scans, compiles a contour map of the area it has been traveling over. It compares these readings with a "map" prepared from reconnaissance data and stored in a computer and correlates the two to determine its location and track. Another possiblity, which could be used over water, detects and records variations in the Earth's magnetic field and uses them for guidance.

Eventually, missiles may be developed that do not show up on radar detection systems or that contain devices to confuse any detector. Either of these developments may render various missile defense systems obsolete.

Lasers, already being developed for guidance systems, are now being considered for use as a weapon. The Pentagon will decide in the next few years whether these "death rays" can be used as practical weapons. One long-range use envisioned for lasers has been as space weapons that could melt satellites or strategic missiles.

Another trend that has important implications for the future of warfare is individually carried weapons. A single soldier can now carry a weapon that is capable of shooting down an aircraft or disabling a tank. Improvements on these are expected in the years ahead.

Other trends involve the use of chemical and biological warfare and the deployment of robots. The use of chemical or biological weapons has, since the end of World War II, been ruled illegal for use in combat; but it is believed by many that they are still stockpiled and that new and more exotic types are being developed and tested. Science fiction has often portrayed robots used in military practice and these cannot be ruled out as potentially effective weapons in a future conflict. The more sophisticated ones may be capable of causing mass destruction, possibly aided by laser technology, and they may have the ability, within a certain degree, to repair themselves.

A few final trends, perhaps the most bizarre, include manipulation of the weather, either in the long run to alter climate or in the short run to create hurricanes and earthquakes. Eventually, the time may come when gravity can be manipulated to achieve the objectives of warfare, either by neutralizing it or otherwise directing it.

Balance of Terror

No characteristic of the current arms race defines it as sharply as overkill—the nuclear capability of exceeding that necessary to destroy the adversary. The United States alone now has enough nuclear bombs stockpiled to equal 615 thousand Hiroshima bombs. This is enough to equal two or three tons of TNT for every person on Earth. It has been reported by the Center for Defense Information, under the direction of Rear Admiral Gene R. La Rocque, that the United States has thirty-five strategic nuclear weapons for every Soviet city over a hundred thousand. The Soviet Union has twenty-eight strategic weapons for every American city over a hundred thousand. Such statistics stimulates many to wonder which nation has superiority. Others, including a number of military analysts believe that since the advent of overkill, the question becomes rather meaningless.

The United States has more strategic bombs and warheads than the Soviet Union with theirs being more powerful but less accurate. In comparing the United States and its North Atlantic Treaty Organization (NATO) allies with the Soviet Union's Warsaw Pact allies, the United States has a quantitative advantage in terms of missiles, bombers, aircraft carriers, and bases. The United States also has a qualitative advantage due to greater combat experience and a wide lead in technological fields such as miniaturization, accuracy, and the ability to survive an attack.

The Soviet Union has twice as many ground forces as the United States, but nearly half of them are engaged in essentially civilian work or assigned to positions not directly threatening to the United States, such as guarding the border with the People's Republic of China. The Soviets have more ships in their navy, but the United States' fleet is more powerful when measured overall tonnage, manpower, or total cost. The Soviets spend a greater percentage of their Gross National Product (GNP) on military expenditures than does the United States, but its total GNP is about half that of the United States.

Most advocates of greater defense spending admit such findings but base their beliefs on trends. They contend that the Soviet Union is increasing their efforts and that the United States should therefore continue to move ahead. Unfortunately, this is the reasoning that has kept the arms race going. It should be remembered that the United States was the first to develop the atomic bomb, the hydrogen bomb, the intercontinental bomb, effective intercontintental ballistic missiles, modern nuclear-powered strategic submarines, and multiple warheads for missiles. Regardless of who is perceived to be ahead, one cannot help wondering when and how such "advances" will end.

Arms Distribution

This tremendous buildup of weapons, both in quantity and power, is now being joined by another form of proliferation; nuclear weapons and the technology to produce them is emerging in an increasing number of nations. The expansion of the "nuclear club" is becoming a grave threat to global security.

Experts forecast that within the next decade about thirty-five countries could have a form of the atomic bomb. Some of these nations have a history of conflict between themselves and other nations. By forecasting the number of nuclear reactors in developing nations, it has been estimated that by 1990 enough plutonium will be produced for approximately three thousand bombs a year.

A further aspect of proliferation is that of conventional weapons sold between nations. The growth of sales has risen rapidly and consistently since World War II, and in 1975 ninety-five nations imported major weapons such as missiles, tanks, aircraft, and ships. Of particular concern is that some of the major buyers are nations that are politically unstable.

Toward Peace

History has not proven favorable in the quest for a less threatening world. Despite nearly continuous attempts to reach agreements, the last three decades have witnessed a tremendous growth in armaments. Arms control negotiations are aimed at stabilizing levels of armaments, whereas disarmament negotiations are aimed at reducing arms to a point where only sufficient arms are retained to enable the nations to maintain domestic tranquility.

Robert C. Johansen of the Institute for World Order has outlined the range of issues that may hold the most promise for a disarmed world:

1. *Banning all nuclear testing.* Partial agreements have been

met but they still allow underground testing.

2. *Establishing nuclear-weapon-free zones.* These regions of the globe would be sanctuaries where no nuclear weapons exist and where nuclear powers agree not to use nuclear weapons.

3. *Limiting strategic arms.* Previous agreements have specified reductions in the number of strategic vehicles, but these are offset by improving their accuracy or adding more warheads to the remaining ones. It is proposed that the superpowers agree to reduce the number of strategic delivery vehicles by a set percentage per year.

4. *Prohibiting tests of new missiles.* Impose a ban on missile flight testing for vehicles with a range beyond six hundred kilometers.

5. *Stopping the proliferation of nuclear weapons.* Going beyond a limit on testing, this proposal calls for a denuclearization of nations that presently possess nuclear arms. In the past, concern has mainly centered on possession of arms by additional governments.

6. *Restricting the use of nuclear weapons.* All nations that possess nuclear weapons would be asked to pledge never to launch weapons against non-nuclear-weapons nations. A second pledge would be to never use nuclear weapons first. The first commitment would reduce the spread of nuclear weapons and the second would act to stabilize relations during a possible war between nuclear-equipped nations.

7. *Prohibiting incendiary weapons.* This provision would restrict conventional weapons, such as naplam, which cause excessive injury and indiscriminate effects.

8. *Prohibiting chemical weapons.* The use of such weapons was banned in 1925, but the research, development, manufacture, and stockpiling of them continues.

9. *Curtailing international arms transfers.* Any agreement is not likely until the major suppliers agree to reduce their own deployment.

10. *Reducing military expenditures.* Nations would agree to reduce their military expenditures by a given percentage each year.

Constraints to a New World Order

While the majority of humankind may agree that the magnitude of these concerns requires attention and that the resolution of them is urgent, it often seems naive to expect governments to take the steps necessary to build a feasible world order. Serious efforts to identify the wider global destiny rather than the national destiny may be met with resistance. The standard operating procedure of many wealthy and more powerful actors in the present world system is either to sustain or reform structures which tend to reinforce the status quo along with its great economic imbalances. Any significant progress toward the realization of a world order is often viewed as threatening by leaders who identify their own well-being with the perpetuation of the present world system.

There is a tendency for governments to become dominated by short-run internal and regional conflicts and poorer nations to compete for aid from the developed world which often acts to perpetuate norms that run counter to the aims of a world order. True, the rhetoric of harmony may induce marginal progress; but the greatest energy and resources, both material and human, go toward sustaining the war system, patterns of domination, and the endless pursuit of wealth, power, and prestige. It is seen as essential to "play the game" and either become a "winner" or a "loser."

Finally, and perhaps of greatest importance, is the inability to transcend the constraints of ideology, nationalism, race, class, and religion. Ethnocentrism is deep-rooted and prevalent throughout the world and may act as the most inpenetrable obstacle inhibiting the realization of a world order.

Constraints on arms reduction can be summarized as

follows:

- National security is still equated with military security.
- Military strength, particularly nuclear, seems to confer prestige and esteem on nations and their leaders.
- Excessive secrecy leads to an atmosphere of mutual fear and distrust which contributes to the spiralling arms race.
- New weapons end up being "bargaining chips" in disarmament talks. When this fails, they are often further developed.

Constraints on the maximization of social and economic well-being include:

- It is difficult to define poverty for both developed and developing nations. A nation may enjoy a steadily rising Gross National Product while the poor segments of its population may experience a worsening of conditions.
- Human needs vary with the climate, ideology, economic organization, and value structure of varius societies.
- Foreign aid is often given as an expression of exploitation, intervention, and/or manipulation.
- Measures of exploitation and dependence are difficult to establish due to lack of data and the vagueness of the concepts themselves.

Constraints on the realization of fundamental human rights and conditions of political justice include:

- Genocide is difficult to define. For example, should the idea of genocide be extended to matters of ideological position?

Constraints on the maintenance and rehabilitation of ecological quality include:

- Infringements on the heritage of humankind with respect to the preservation of cultural or national wonders or with regard to the conservation of endangered animal species require international mechanisms that assert global concern and gives hard-pressed governments an incentive to protect them without inhibiting the satisfaction of fundamental human needs.

● Most ecological issues require extensive information, intergovernmental coordination, and the development of ethical attitudes.

Questions for Discussion

1. Is world security eroding? What is world security?

2. Does humankind demonstrate its greatest ingenuity in developing military technology?

3. Is brotherhood a precondition for survival?

4. Is there any danger in the quest for world order?

5. Do you think you will fight a war in your lifetime?

6. What are other trends in military technology?

7. Should nations export nuclear technology?

8. Do you agree with the ten issues that may hold the most promise for a disarmed world? Should others be added?

9. Are there other constraints to the maximization of world order? How can they be overcome?

Activities

1. Write a scenario for World War III.

2. You are in charge of diverting substantial military related funds to other areas of the economy. Outline your priorities.

3. Brainstorm ways to reduce the arms race.

4. Construct a futures wheel centered on increased armaments.

Primary Sources

Brown, Lester R. *World Without Borders.* New York: Random House, 1972.

Falk, Richard A. *A Study of Future Worlds.* New York: The Free Press, 1975.

Falk, Richard A. *This Endangered Planet: Prospects and Proposals for Human Survival.* New York: Random House, 1972.

Falk, Richard A., and Black, Cyril E. *The Future of the International Legal Order.* Princeton, N.J.: Princeton University Press, 1972.

Laszlo, Ervin. *A Strategy for the Future.* New York: George Braziller, 1974.

Laszlo, Ervin, et. al. *Goals for Mankind: A Report to the Club of Rome.* New York: E.P. Dutton, 1977.

Mendlovitz, Saul H. *On the Creation of a Just World Order.* New York: The Free Press, 1975.

Preview

After centuries of scientific reasoning, scientists are only now giving us an awareness of the tiny molecular building blocks of which we are made and of the enormous and perhaps infinite universe we live in. In 1957 the satellite Sputnik, the first satellite launched, ushered in a new era. Four years later, Yuri Gagarin of the Soviet Union photographed our planet from orbit, and eight years after that Neil Armstrong, Edwin Aldrin, and Mike Collins of the United States televised their exploration of the Moon a quarter of a million miles from Earth. Edwin Aldrin writes:

Twelve men have now walked on the Moon. The twelve of us have, I think, at least one common viewpoint: We share a special concept of the Earth as a planet. We have looked on it from the surface of the Moon and seen it whole in space—beautiful, bright, not very large . . . and somehow vulnerable. To me it seemed a great place to come from, and an even greater place to return to. Millions now have had a reflection of this view of Earth through the dramatic photographs taken in space; I think they too begin to share this sense of planet Earth as a place to cherish, and even are beginning to act upon it. (*Our World in Space.* New York: Graphic Society, 1974.)

CHAPTER 12

THE UNIVERSE

Satellites

In addition to their pure scientific value, satellites have, over the last twenty years, had a large effect upon everyday life. They have revolutionized our entire communications systems as well as contributing to meterology, resource studies, and other applications.

The following outline highlights some of the present applications of satellite technology as well as some which are expected to be developed by 1990:

Earth Observations

Climate and Weather
- Accurate long-term forecasts
- Early storm warnings
- Rapid, dependable service
- Precipitation control
- Fog dispersal
- Hail suppression

Environmental Quality
- Pollution intensity, identification, and dispersal

Water Conservation

Mineral Prospecting

Ocean
- Sea ice, location and movement
- Nutrient-rich fish-attracting areas
- Tides, currents
- Variations in chlorophyll

Crops and Forest Features
● Species and damage (insects, fires)
Provide Surface Maps
● Landforms, field patterns
● Geological features
● Coastline details
Discriminate Surface Features
● Natural geological formations
● Man-made objects

Communication Networks
Medical Purposes
Business and Commerce
Education
Disaster Warning
Search and Rescue

Solar Energy
Solar power satellites could collect concentrated solar energy and beam it to converter station sites on earth.

It has been proposed that satellites be used to maintain a public (meaning the whole world) inventory of all military activity everywhere on Earth. This would supplement the intelligence systems used by individual nations and serve to limit the proliferation of weapons and safeguard against an accidental war.

Satellites will play an expanded role in the future with many of them being placed in permanent orbits and regularly serviced in space. Others will be sent up for specific tasks and brought down when completed.

Skylab

The Skylab Project of the early seventies provided a great deal of information about human capabilities to operate in space. Three missions, each composed of three men, existed in space sequentially for periods of twenty-eight days, fifty-nine days, and eighty-four days.

Perhaps the single most important lesson learned from the project was that it is possible to support a human being in space for as long as eighty-four days. It was found that three conditions were necessary for the comfort, well-being, and productiveness of the crew members. They must have sufficient food at regular intervals, enough sleep at appropriate times, and exercise at regular intervals.

There were some adverse physiological reactions in spite of this including a loss of blood volume, motion sickness, degeneration of certain bones, loss of bone marrow, and a slackening of muscle tone. It was also discovered that because of the weightlessness encountered in space the heart does not have to pump as hard as on Earth to circulate the blood. As a result the muscles of the heart become weak and when subjected to the gravity of Earth a severe strain is put upon the returning space traveler. Studies are now being conducted to further understand the relationship between the length of time spent in weightlessness and how long it takes the cardiovascular system to return to its original condition.

Space Shuttle

During the next decade the Space Shuttle will constitute the National Aeronautics and Space Administration's (NASA's) major single effort to realize the nation's broad objectives in space. It will usher in a new era in space by serving as a bridge to future activities, both manned and unmanned.

The Shuttle is a reusable vehicle which will be used as a transportation system in low Earth orbit for a wide variety of missions. It is a manned spacecraft, but unlike previous craft it will land like an airplane and can be used many times over. Thus it is estimated to be able to carry out a variety of assignments for a fraction of the current cost per pound of payload.

Destined to become the workhorse of the space program,

the Space Shuttle is a true aerospace vehicle. It takes off like a rocket, maneuvers in orbit like a spacecraft, and lands like an airplane. This versatility will enable it to perform a variety of functions. Among its first missions will be to inspect and repair unmanned satellites in orbit or return them to Earth if necessary. The Shuttle may also be used to deploy a telescope observatory which will be used in Earth orbit unhindered by atmospheric distortion.

In addition to these functions, the Shuttle is scheduled to carry a complete scientific laboratory into Earth orbit. The Spacelab will remain attached to the shuttle throughout its seven to thirty day mission. Spacelab is an example of international cooperation as it was developed and will be used by personnel from many nations and different backgrounds.

It is foreseen that eventually the Space Shuttle or a version of it will transport people to different locations on Earth or, if taken into orbit, may serve as a space hotel. At some point vacationers may even choose to go to the Moon via Space Shuttle.

Within a few years after the program is developed, it is believed that a Space Tug will be needed. The Tug will be capable of retrieval by the Shuttle to enable its return to Earth and subsequent reuse. Used in this manner, the large vehicle will provide an effective means to support the entire spectrum of possible future missions.

Space Benefits

Once a space program or particular mission is completed, the scientific or engineering goals are not necessarily terminated. It is becoming increasingly apparent that humankind can benefit from space activities in many ways by utilizing what is known as spinoff technology. It is through such technology that we are beginning to realize the relevance of space to human concerns. These concerns fall into three broad categories: health care, Earth resources, and safety.

Health Care

● Blood pressure and heart monitors so small they can be inserted by a hypodermic needle rather than surgery.

● Sterilization methods to keep operating rooms infection-free.

● Remote monitoring equipment that allows one nurse to keep a continual check on sixty-four patients at once.

● Wheelchairs that quadriplegics can control with voice commands.

● Control switches operated by eye movement for paralyzed patients.

● A suitcase-sized emergency treatment kit for ambulance attendants.

● Easy-to-prepare meals for senior citizens based on space food processing techniques.

● A bioisolation garment which allows immunity-deficient children to carry a germ-free environment around with them.

Earth Resources

● All the benefits previously covered under satellites.

Safety

● Fire-resistant fabrics for firefighter protection, aircraft interiors, and upholstery and drapery materials for the home.

Other spinoffs include ballpoint pens that write in any position, miniature tape recorders, and instant reservation and computer systems.

Lunar Exploration

Humankind's greatest technological achievement took place on July 16, 1969 when Neil Armstrong set foot on the Moon. Perhaps the most important contribution of the

166

Apollo missions was showing that humans can successfully travel to and from the lunar surface and can remain there for at least short periods of time. With further study of reduced gravity and advanced spacesuit technology, the length of stay will be extended.

The full significance of the lunar data acquired during the last decade will not be known for many years, but it is apparent that further exploration and scientific study of the moon will greatly add to our knowledge of the universe. There is thus great interest in establishing a permanent base on the Moon.

One of the ultimate goals of a lunar base would be to make it as self-sufficient as possible. It now appears possible that solar energy could be used to derive hydrogen and oxygen from lunar material which could then be used for fuel and making water. Indoor farming could grow food, roving vehicles could provide transportation, and observatories could facilitate further study of the space environment. The venture could become more economically viable if it were used to help construct solar power satellites. A large percentage of the cost of such satellites, if constructed on Earth, would be spent to transport it from the surface to its final orbit. It would cost only one-twentieth of the energy to put it into orbit from the Moon. Hopefully this endeavor would be accomplished as a joint venture through the cooperation of various nations.

Space Colonies

The developments that have been discussed so far, from the first satellite to human lunar exploration and the possiblitity of establishing moon bases, may all be leading to the ultimate in human space endeavors—the colonizing of the heavens.

Philosophers as well as scientists have often agreed that civilization cannot continue to exist without new frontiers. The need is both physical and spiritual. It seems that humans have always longed for adventure, diversity, novelty, and romance. At a time when virtually the entire Earth has been explored, the road to the stars may be discovered noon too soon. the space frontier is limitless; the opportunity and challenge is beyond exhaustion and both are totally different from what has ever been experienced before.

Not only is the spiritual aspect to be considered, but according to Professor Gerard K. O'Neill, a Princeton University physicist, the physical needs are immediate. These include a need to solve the energy crisis and, in a longer time perspective, the problem of population and Earth's capacity to support it. Related to these are the availability of food and living space both of which are becoming increasingly scarce.

O'Neill believes that our only hope is to find a cheap, inexhaustible, universally available energy source but that this cannot be achieved by any means developed on Earth—at least not without disastrous environmental consequences. One of the major objectives of space colonization would be to build large solar power stations in orbit which would convert the power to microwave energy and then direct it in a narrow beam to fixed antennas on Earth. This would be more efficient than fossil fuels and produce no radioactive wastes as nuclear power currently does. The construction of solar-power stations for Earth would then be the first industry for space colonies.

It is further pointed out by proponents of space colonization that we are running out of raw materials. The Earth contains abundant quantities of essential metals, but beyond a certain point it will be impossible to extract them without doing intolerable damage to the environment. The Apollo findings indicate that the Moon could be a rich source of industrial materials including silicon, aluminum, iron, magnesium, and titanium. At a future time we may begin to exploit the resources of the asteroid belts which are rich in carbon, nitrogen, and hydrogen.

Also the colonization of space will enable us to reduce the strain of population growth on our planet. Statistics are often cited which point to a future of massive overpopulation and all the problems associated with this. While this may be the case, it should be pointed out that many people feel that space colonization, while having many attributes, cannot in any way act to substantially alleviate this problem. Even a migration of hundreds of thousands would not appreciably reduce the burden of overpopulation; and, if the colonists were to utilize the raw materials of space, the Earth-bound people would still be dependent on their own resources.

In spite of this, the prospect of humanizing the universe may still provide our civilization with abundant energy and spiritual renewal. Even if no physical relief is given to a congested and impoverished Earth, the intellectual and emotional contribution may prove to be enormous. Ultimately, after 4.5 billion years, it may prove to be the only link to the continued evolution of our species.

Universe Exploration

In the early 1960's, Mariner 2 came within twenty-two thousand miles of Venus and sent back to Earth information from this alien world. Since then we have launched vehicles to Mars, Jupiter, and Mercury, and it is forseeable that by the end of this century these probes will reach to the very boundary of our solar system.

This raises an important question: Why are we exploring these distant worlds? We are doing it as a means to attempt to answer some very fundamental questions. They include the following:

- What is the universe?
- What are pulsars, quasars, and black holes?
- How did the solar system originate and evolve?
- What are the other planets like?
- What can study of the solar system tell us about Earth?

● Does life exist elsewhere?

The Viking missions to Mars in 1975-1977 serve as an example of the primary objectives of most space probes. First and most important is the search for living organisms and, if detected, an examination of their nature. Second is an analysis of the composition of the surface. Third is to measure the atmospheric temperature, pressure, and wind direction and velocity. The fourth objective is to examine the planet structure, chemistry, and topography.

It is believed by many scientists that in the comparatively near future the entire solar system will be explored by sophisticated unmanned space vehicles. In the 1980's and 1990's probes will be made into the atmospheres of Jupiter and Saturn, perhaps planets as distant as Neptune and Pluto and even Sun probes which will radio data back to Earth before melting.

Further into the future it is forecast that human voyages may be made which, due to the tremendous distances, may last for years or even centuries and that suspended animation of the astronauts may be called for. If vehicles could travel the speed of light, the theory of relativity indicates that time would pass more slowly for the astronauts. A less exotic method of deep space penetration may be possible by using self-contained vehicles that would permit journeys lasting generation after generation.

Rendezvous with a Comet

A mission to rendezvous with the famous Halley's comet was planned by NASA. Coming close to the Sun in 1986, it was the only opportunity for scientists of this generation to study it because it will not return for another seventy-six years.

Scientists have long wanted to sample the comets because they suspect they contain surviving bits of primitive matter out of which the solar system has evolved.

The proposed mission would have sent a probe into it when the comet was 93 million miles from Earth. The spacecraft would have then moved on to a second comet, Temple 2, and possible dock on it to obtain samples. But lack of sufficient funds prevented the rendezvous by NASA.

The idea that there may be life in other areas of the universe has, after centuries of unimaginative disinterest, finally come of age. It is an area that has now reached a practical stage and is being pursued by rigorous scientific methods.

The evolution of life on Earth is the result of random events in which small differences early in the process have a profound significance in latter stages. With all these random factors operating over a period of five billion years, it seems unlikely that organisms of a different environment of another planet would resemble human beings. It would seem incredible that we alone have made such steps to intelligent life for we are only one planet circling one of the hundred billion other stars in our galaxy.

Due to breakthroughs in electronics it appears that the the greater part of our search for extraterrestrial life will be by radio. Only a few years ago this would have seemed absurd, but now we have receivers of such sensitivity and antennas of such enormous size that we can hope to pick up signals from the nearest stars—if they are being sent out.

It must be remembered that any electromagnetic vibration, including radio waves, moves at the speed of light which is 186,000 miles (or 300,000 kilometers) per second. This means that any knowledge sent or received will be out of date as a result of the tremendous distances involved. For example, if we were to pick up a signal from a planet circling a star in the Andromeda Spiral, we would know that intelligence existed there about two *million* years ago because that is when the signal would have been sent. Radio was developed on Earth about seventy-five years ago so that, from the point of view of an alien civilization lying more than seventy-five light years away from us, we are still "radio quiet"; our transmissions have not yet penetrated farther into the galaxy.

Our first serious attempt to communicate with extraterrestrial civilization occurred in 1972 when Pioneer 10 was launched. It was the first vehicle to leave the solar system—its velocity was about seven miles per second. A gold-anodized aluminum plaque, six inches by nine inches, is attached to the antenna and is intended as a pictorial greeting to interstellar beings. It is written in the language of science and intends to communicate the location, era, and something of the nature of human beings; but it may be a while before any results are seen since Pioneer 10 could not reach the nearest star in less than eighty *thousand* years. It is predicted then that any contact will first be made by radio signals long before we meet extraterrestrial beings face to face.

The search for extraterrestrial life by means of radio messages and space vehicles indicates that most scientists agree that there are other intelligent beings in the universe. It is believed that, with sufficient time and an environment that allows change, it is improbable that the Earth is the only inhabited planet in a universe containing billions of possible habitats.

As our scientific knowledge continues to expand, we have begun to contemplate endeavors which may change human history. We have known for some time that Venus, with its dreadful environment, would simultaneously fry, crush, suffocate, and blind any human inhabitants. This is due to the rich atmosphere of carbon dioxide (CO_2). Venus could be made livable if only the carbon dioxide could be split into its two components: carbon (C) and oxygen (O_2). With this in mind, Dr. Carl Sagan, Director of the Laboratory for

172

Planetary Studies at Cornell University, has proposed one of the boldest schemes that humankind has ever contemplated. In order to break down carbon dioxide as plants do on Earth through photosynthesis, Dr. Sagan suggests we introduce blue-green algae into the atmosphere of Venus. It is very hardy, reproduces rapidly, and attacks carbon dioxide and separates it into its individual components. Eventually, the temperature of the lower atmosphere will decrease and rain will be produced. The entire scheme would require no more than about a dozen orbiting spacecraft and a few thousand small algae rockets to begin the process of redesigning Venus. This biological process would, of course, take thousands of years before any dramatic changes could be seen.

Establishing the existence of extraterrestrial life or making another planet habitable for humans would surely rank as one of the major breakthroughs of science for either of these events would radically alter the philosophical and religious beliefs of humankind.

Questions for Discussion

1. What might Edwin Aldren have meant when he said that the Earth looked vulnerable?

2. Will satellites someday be used by an international organization to monitor all military activities to limit warfare?

3. What role will the Space Shuttle play in future space programs?

4. Can human civilization continue without new frontiers?

5. Would you like to be a space colonist? Why or why not?

6. Should we attempt to make Venus habitable for human life?

7. Many people believe we should not spend millions of dollars on a space program when we have so many problems at home. Do you agree?

8. How does the military now use space and how might it do so in the future?

9. Who should own the planets in our solar system?

10. Was our reaching the Moon the greatest technological accomplishment to date?

Activities

1. Write a speech condemning the space program on the grounds that we cannot afford it.

2. Write a speech in support of the space program on the grounds that it is necessary and not a luxury.

3. Brainstorm all the possible examples of spinoff technology from the space program that may be developed in the future.

4. Produce a travel brochure for the Shuttle Hotel and Resort.

5. Write a scenario on what a first day in a space colony would be like.

6. The Secretary-General of the United Nations has asked you to write a speech that he can keep in his files in the event of an extraterrestrial visit. Write the speech.

Primary Resources

A Compendium of Future Space Activities. Program Planning Office, Lyndon B. Johnson Space Center, Houston, Texas (Sept. 1977).

Cole, Dandridge M. *Beyond Tomorrow: The Next 50 Years in Space.* Amherst, Wisconsin: Amherst Press, 1965.

O'Neil, Gerard K. *The High Frontier: Human Colonies in Space.* New York: William Morrow & Co., 1977.

Paine, Thomas O. "What Lies Ahead in Space?" *The Futurist* Vol. V (April 1971).

Sagan, Carl. *The Cosmic Connection: An Extraterrestrial Perspective.* New York: Dell Publishing Co., 1973.

Preview

While interest in the future is nearly as old as human civilization, we are now witnessing a tremendous surge of activity with an eye toward the future. Why is this occurring? One reason may be that many feel as though they are seated in a plane listening to the following announcement:

> Good afternoon ladies and gentlemen. This is your pilot speaking. We are flying at an altitude of 35,000 feet and a speed of 700 miles per hour. I have two pieces of news to report, one good and one bad. The bad news is that we are lost. The good news is that we are making excellent time.

There are many rationales for studying the future, many of them stemming from anxiety, some merely from interest, but all from hope—hope that by planning our future, we may survive it.

Teachers in all levels, from primary grades to the university level, are orienting their educational experiences toward the future for we all have a stake in it and education plays a primary role in shaping the future. Various government agencies, ranging from the military to public health, are utilizing the tools and images of futures research in order to more effectively perform their tasks. The private sector, whether it be a large multinational corporation or a small local business, are recognizing the need to anticipate and adapt to future change. Individuals of all ages and all walks of life are beginning to take profound interest in the rest of their lives and the lives of future generations.

This chapter briefly describes some of the organizations and individuals that have contributed to the field. It would be impossible to include all that deserve attention, but it is hoped that what follows will encourage further investigation and, more importantly, participation; for, as C.F. Kettering said, "My interest is in the future, because I'm going to spend the rest of my life there."

CHAPTER 13

FUTURES-ORIENTED ORGANIZATIONS
World Future Society

The largest futures-oriented organization, the World Future Society, is an association of people interested in future societal and technological developments and operates on a nonprofit basis.

The Society's objectives, as stated in its charter, are as follows:

1. To contribute to a reasoned awareness of the future and the importance of its study, without advocating particular ideologies or engaging in political activities.

2. To advance responsible and serious investigations of the future.

3. To promote the development and improvement of methodologies for the study of the future.

4. To increase public understanding of future-oriented activities and studies.

5. To facilitate communication and cooperation among organizations and individuals interested in studying or planning for the future.

The major publication of the Society is *The Futurist: A Journal of Forecasts, Trends, and Ideas about the Future.* Other publications deal specifically with such topics as government, business, communications, health, technology, education, and others.

Local chapters which offer speakers, educational courses, seminars, and discussion groups have developed in over one hundred cities around the world. Membership into the World

Future Society is open to anyone who is seriously interested in the future, and there presently are more than 25,000 members in over eighty nations.

The RAND Corporation and the Hudson Institute

The Cold War, during the 1950's and 1960's, was a period of insecurity for the United States and tremendous amounts of money were poured into the nation's defense. In order to carry out the task, it was necessary to orient much of our technological research toward the future.

In 1946 the Douglas Aircraft Company, in cooperation with the Air Force, established Project RAND (an acronym for *R*esearch and *D*evelopment). The original intent was to study aerial intercontinental warfare. Two years later, Project RAND split off from Douglas, and the RAND Corporation was formed. This new organization expanded its investigations to include more general policies of the nation and not just weaponry systems.

Methods of studying the future were developed, including the Delphi technique which is used to create a consensus forecast on a specific future development. Not to remain unique for long, the RAND Corporation gave birth to a host of other research organizations or "think tanks"— organizations that conduct research for private corporations, agencies of the government, or other institutions.

One of these is the Hudson Institute founded in 1961 by Herman Kahn. To speak of one without the other would be difficult, and many critics of the Institute suggest that it is simply an extension of Kahn, in spite of the fact that the Institute now employs about fifty permanent staff and one hundred consultants.

For many years Kahn was best known for his book *On Thermonuclear War* published in 1960. A second book, published in 1962, entitled *Thinking about the Unthinkable* was also about the need to speculate about the possibilities and results of nuclear war. Since then his interests have shifted from military affairs to more general studies of the future. In 1967, he and Anthony J. Wiener wrote *The Year 2000: A Framework for Speculation on the Next Thirty-Three Years.* This large volume was the first of his works dealing with broad issues of the future.

Another major publication came in 1976 and was co-authored with William Brown and Leon Martel. *The Next 200 Years: A Scenario for America and the World* is most noted for its optimism. In spite of its title, which was chosen because of the United States' Bicentennial, the scope of the work is mainly focused on the next fifty years. Kahn and his co-authors foresee a future of increased affluence, with pollution and the depletion of natural resources being solved by improved technology. Considerable debate has been generated by the book, particularly from those that think it is overly optimistic.

The Institute for World Order

Founded in 1948, the Institute for World Order is involved in promoting the values of peace, social justice, economic well-being, and ecological balance through research and education. It seeks to develop an awareness of the need for new systems of social/political/economic institutions built on human values. In order to do this the members analyze world problems and attempt to initiate public discussion of these issues with the hope of eventually mobilizing political constituencies toward these goals.

A transnational research enterprise, the World Order Models Project (WOMP), emerging originally as an effort to eliminate war as a human social institution was begun in 1966. The result was a series of five volumes entitled *Preferred Worlds for the 1990s.* Each author was asked to diagnose the

178

contemporary world order system based on what each perceived as a preferred or desirable world order and strategies of transition to the new order.

Presently the Institute is working on the "Lodi Project," with the objective of creating a single composite model based on the earlier series of works. At the same time, the Institute is also working on political strategies for this decade to help get its model implemented.

Center for Integrative Studies

The primary focus of the Center for Integrative Studies is on the long-range social and cultural implications in society, with a strong emphasis on global trends. The aims of the Center are:

1. To analyze and project the large-scale future consequences of social, cultural, and technological trends in ways that may provide a more holistic framework for their appraisal.

2. To function as a sensing and alerting unit concerned with the effects of changes on the quality of the human environment and with the identification of critical issues which may emerge as focal points for present and future decisions.

3. To explore and formulate guidelines for the study and evaluation of future developments, particularly at the international level, with emphasis on their long-range consequences for, and impacts upon, different socieites and social groups.

The Club of Rome

In 1967, Aurelio Peccei, an Italian industrialist and economist, met with Alexander King, a French scientist and global analyst. They discussed the present world system which they believed to be "a textbook case of mismanagement" resulting from overpopulation, starvation, pollution, poverty, depletion of resources, etc. A year later they invited thirty persons representing ten countries to meet in Rome. The Club of Rome was formed and is today a highly exclusive association of scientists, economists, industrialists, and educators, with a membership limited to one hundred.

The purpose of the Club is to stimulate political action that will influence world affairs in a rational and humane direction. Wide public recognition was achieved soon after the Project on the Predicament of Mankind was initiated. Under the direction of Professor Dennis L. Meadows, a group of scholars at the Massachusetts Institute of Technology (MIT) began examining the complex of global problems using computers to simulate world trends and where they might lead. The computerized mathematical "model" was developed by Professor Jay W. Forrester and the Systems Dynamics Group at MIT. The model deals with five components of the world situation: population, industrialization, food supply, depletion of nonrenewable resources and pollution. Together these form what the Club of Rome calls the "world problematique." Data centered on these components were fed into a computer which generated projections of what may occur in the future, depending upon different assumptions about each of the components.

In 1972 the study resulted in a book, *The Limits to Growth,* by Dennis Meadows, Donella Meadows, Jorgen Randers, and W.W. Behrens III. It has sold three million copies and has appeared in thirty-four languages.

Almost immediately the book stirred controversy with critics arguing that it is overly pessimistic, that the methods were biased, and that such a broad and complex study could not be reduced to a computer simulation. The authors had, from its inception, stated that their work was experimental and was offered as a base for further research. The debate has come to be one of the most important issues in the futures field—the "limits to growth" question. Essentially the question is: Can the world's economy continue to grow at its present rate without causing great disorder within the next decades? The book's message was that, given present trends, the global system probably cannot support itself beyond approximately the year 2100.

The club of Rome's second report, *Mankind at the Turning Point* by Mihajlo Mesarovic and Eduard Pestel, used a more sophisticated computer model and divided the world into ten regions. The study concentrated on two great gaps—one between humans and nature and the second between the developed nations in the northern part of the world and the developing countries in the southern portions. The authors concluded that a complete halt to growth was undesirable and instead advocated "organic" growth which would be selective and more critically managed than unrestrained growth. This will allow the developing nations to improve their lives but only if the wealthier nations act to conserve resources.

By the mid-1970's, the Club of Rome was sponsoring a number of projects, all within a global context. While the earlier works had focused on problems of poor global economic planning and unlimited economic growth, a new project took a different approach. The result, written by Professor Ervin Laszlo and others, was entitled *Goals for Mankind,* with attention being given to the human element. Following this orientation, differing cultural attitudes and values within individuals, groups, and nations were investigated in relation to the specified goals of various regions, nations, and organizations. It was recognized that change might not happen fast enough to bring about a creative and humanistic transformation to a more desirable world order but that mutual awareness of intentions or goals may be beneficial.

In 1976 a further report, entitled *Reshaping the International Order,* was coordinated by Jan Tinbergen, a Dutch economist. The objective was to outline new global arrangements in the hope of ensuring a life of dignity for everyone in the world. The book proposes a number of steps, including the establishment of an international monetary system, arms reduction, and global resource management.

The latest report, *No Limits to Learning: Bridging the Human Gap,* stresses that learning and the individual human being, rather than material resources, are the key to the world's future.

Presently, the Club of Rome is initiating other projects involving scholars from many nations, including developing ones. Regardless of specific activities, the people involved with the Club all agree on the underlying recognition that the world needs to change its social and political structures if catastrophe is to be avoided.

Worldwatch Institute

The Worldwatch Institute, headed by Lester Brown, author of *World Without Borders,* was establishe in 1973 and seeks to anticipate global problems and social trends through an international approach that cuts across traditional disciplines. The Institute's projects include:

● Global energy alternatives, with particular emphasis on possibilities for conservation and on the development of safe, renewable energy sources.

● Environmentally induced illnesses: the effect of lifestyles, diet, pollutants, stress, poverty, under-nutrition, and over-nutrition on health.

● The changing status cf women: its impact on politics, economics, and society.

● Current global trends in population growth, family planning, and the many dimensions of the population problem.

● Economic, political, and demographic discontinuities facing the world in the last quarter of this century.

Primary Sources

Botkin, James W., Elmandjra, M., and Malitza, M. *No Limits to Learning: Bridging the Human Gap.* Elmsford, NY: Pergamon, 1979.

Kahn, Herman. *The Next 200 Years: A Scenario for America and the World.* New York: William Morrow and Co., 1976.

Meadows, Donella H. and Dennis L.; Randers, Jorgen; and Behrens, William W. III. *The Limits to Growth.* New York: Universe Books, 1974.

Mesarovik, Mihajlo, and Pestel, Eduard. *Mankind at the Turning Point.* New York: E. P. Dutton, 1974.

Tinbergen, Jan, coordinator. *RIO: Reshaping the International Order.* New York: E. P. Dutton, 1976.

Other Related ETC Titles

Futurecasting - Charting a Way to Your Future: By Joel A. Kurtzman - $9.95

A book to help you shape the future you want to instead of reacting to happenstance events . . . resulting in a future you do not choose.

Making Changes: A futures oriented course in inventive problem solving

By John Thomas — $19.95 (Teacher's Edition) $9.95 (Student's Edition)

". . . a meaningful replacement for the 'life skill competencies' being mandated by state legislatures and school boards. It truly is designed to make children think . . . well conceived, organized, and packaged . . . the materials deserve an over-all rating of 'excellent.'"
— **Educational Technology Publications**

Teaching the Future: A guide to future-oriented education

By Draper L. Kauffman — $14.95 (Hardcover) $9.95 (Softcover)

"Less controversial and more practical than any other publication dealing with future education . . . is well-researched, logical, and lucid . . . offers an extensive bibliography, activities, techniques, and special projects and exercises." — **The United Teacher**

The Future File: A guide for people with one foot in the 21st Century

By Paul Dickson — $12.95

Foundations of Futurology in Education

Edited by Richard W. Hostrop — $12.95

". . . . a unique, disturbing, and important book for all those concerned with the future of education." — **Choice**

Alternative U.S. Futures: A policy analysis of individual choices in a political economy

By Stahrl W. Edmunds — $9.95

The Future: Human ecology and education

By Edward A. Sullivan — $9.95

" . . . account of psychophysiology covers the whole spectrum, with good sections on behavioral control achieved by electrical brain stimulation, chemotherapy, psychosurgery, hypnosis, and biofeedback training. He offers a good review of work which has been done on the biology of violence and physiological means of controlling violent behavior."
— **Phi Delta Kappan**

The Teacher as World Citizen: A scenario of the 21st Century

By Theodore Brameld — $9.95 (Hardcover) $5.95 (Softcover)

Historian W. Warren Wager has called Theodore Brameld a "prophet-father of the coming world civilization." Jack R. Frymier, Editor of the Educational Forum, says in his Foreword to **The Teacher as World Citizen,** "This volume will evoke feelings and provoke thoughts to a greater degree, probably, than almost any book you have ever read."

Education for Transformation: Implications in Lewis & Mumford's Ecohumanism

By David R. Conrad — $14.95

David Conrad, writing in the tradition of Paulo Freire and Ivan Illich, has here advanced the literature of radical philosophy of education by researching and analyzing the prolific writings of Lewis Mumford and then laying out for our discussion their powerful edcuational directives." — **Educational Studies**

The above books, if not found in your bookstore, may be ordered directly from ETC Publications, Palm Springs, CA 92263-1608. Purchase orders, personal checks, Master-Card and VISA acceptable. California residents, please add 6% sales tax. Free shipping on all prepaid orders.